CALL
of an
ANGEL

PATRICIA O'TOOLE

blackbird
blackbird-books.com

For Mum and Dad
Thank you for everything

The Beginning

From a young age I was fascinated by nature and many of my earliest memories are associated with the fate of plants and animals. It didn't seem that a day passed by that I wasn't either rescuing a sick animal or watering a dying plant.

By the age of seven, although I don't remember having many toys, my bedroom was filled with plants of every shape and size, which I cared for lovingly.

I suppose one could call this personal crusade a hobby and that is certainly how I saw it then. But now I know there was much more to this bond with nature and it was through this bond that I first felt the presence of an angel. An angel that came to comfort me in a time of great distress, although at the time I had no understanding of what was happening.

Since then I have seen many angels, but it wasn't until receiving the seemingly innocent present of a gift voucher years later, that I really understood what took place that day.

1

The Unexpected Gift

The story begins in Ireland in 2004. It was Christmas Eve and just as I was leaving work, a colleague slipped an envelope into my hand, wishing me a happy Christmas. Expecting to find the usual festive card inside, I was surprised to find a gift voucher for a shop in my local town. I didn't recognise the name of the shop but decided that on my next trip into town, I would find out where it was and what it sold.

Like many towns in rural Ireland, ours comprises of a small number of scattered yet somehow interlinking streets and it didn't take long to find the shop, hidden down a small alleyway that I seldom used. With a quick peek through the windows, various objects could be seen, such as angels, fairies and elves and I hesitated before going in as I had little interest in such things. Ten minutes later I wasn't surprised to find myself back outside empty handed and that evening I tucked the voucher away in a drawer and totally forgot about it.

About six months later, while having coffee with my

friend, Caroline, she happened to mention a medium who was visiting our town that week. She said the medium was renowned for her amazingly accurate Tarot card readings and that she was thinking of going to see her. When I heard that the readings were being held in the shop to which I had the gift voucher, I thought that this might be the perfect opportunity to use it.

Later that evening I searched through the drawer where I thought I had put the voucher, wondering if it was still even there. Eventually, finding it right at the bottom, I saw it had an expiry date only a week away. So, the next day, ignoring all misgivings, I rang the shop and booked an appointment to see the medium the following morning.

After a quick breakfast and before there could be any change of heart I drove the short distance to town. Once at the shop I was led upstairs to meet the medium, who was sitting in a dimly lit room. I wasn't quite sure how she might look, having never met a medium before, but she certainly didn't seem anything out of the ordinary. Feeling a bit guilty for expecting her to look otherwise, I smiled warmly at her and she introduced herself as Sally.

Once alone, we chatted for a few minutes until she asked me what kind of cards I would like a reading from. Sally showed me various sorts, including Tarot. I have never really liked the idea of Tarot cards so the sight of them was enough to prompt me to say that I didn't want a card reading after all and I asked if there anything else she could do. So, instead of a card reading, Sally asked me to sit close beside her and to hold her hand – which, after a moment's pause, I did. She then put a crystal into her other hand and asked me to close my eyes.

It seems impossible to continue my story without acknowledging that it was at this point my understanding of life began to change. The simplest way to describe what happened would be that of an awakening to another level of consciousness, of which previously I had been unaware. As soon as I closed my eyes, a strange tingling began to run through my body, a sensation that came and went in very strong waves. It travelled up from the hand that Sally was holding and spread throughout my whole body, even into my face. Alarmed by this new sensation, I opened my eyes to tell her. She assured me that it was alright and that it just meant a spirit was coming through to communicate with us, which alarmed me even more.

The thought that ghosts coexist with us had always terrified me and I was certain that if I actually saw one I would pass out with fright. Therefore, to be told that one was travelling up through my hand was nearly enough to send me running back down the stairs and all the way home without a backward glance. However, we continued to sit together as I was somehow aware now that our hands were joined, it was a connection that was not mine to break.

I distinctly remember one presence that Sally described clearly to me. She thought it was a spirit and at the time so did I, since I knew so little, yet I now know that it was an angelic being. Sally described her as being extremely beautiful, a woman with long flowing hair who was exquisitely dressed and who seemed to have a message for me: I was to look for Gretta McCarthy, to whom I was distantly related. This was not a name I was familiar with. Challenging her about this information, she once more made contact with the presence. To my surprise, it replied, saying there were many relatives living near me that I didn't know, but to find this particular one. It was also insistent that I find a specific tree, which, despite being able to see it clearly in her mind, Sally did not recognise.

Afterwards, we chatted about the unusual messages. Sally said she wished she was an artist so that she could capture the beauty of the presence that had appeared to her. Little did either of us know that not only would this presence soon reappear in my life, but many others as well. Sally asked me to call back and tell her if Gretta McCarthy was ever found. Promising that I would, we said our goodbyes.

Intrigued by the whole experience, the morning's events were relayed to my two sons, Lee and Thomas, when I got home. Gretta McCarthy was discussed at some length, especially the fact that she was apparently related to us and yet we had no idea who she was. We also considered whether she was even alive, since the medium could contact spirits. After much debate, we decided to look into nearby church graveyards to see if we could spot the name. It was soon obvious that McCarthy is a very common Irish name and it did not take long to realise that finding the right grave would be impossible. Furthermore, given the bizarre nature of the tale, we couldn't exactly try to enlist the help of the local priest. In the end we gave up our search and once again things were forgotten about.

A festival to remember

It was another friend, Ellen, who unknowingly set the story back in motion. About six months later she rang, asking if I would be interested in going to a Mind, Body & Spirit festival in the nearby city as she had two free tickets. Since I hadn't anything on that particular weekend, I agreed to tag along, although I was not sure what this kind of festival entailed.

Two days later we arrived at the festival, faced with countless number of stands selling a mind-boggling array of alternative therapies. It was an extremely busy scene, and I was soon drawn in by the lively atmosphere. What particularly struck me was the number of people queuing to see mediums or those giving card readings. It reminded me of my visit with Sally back at home. There was so much happening that it was necessary to circuit the entire event several times to take it all in. On my third time around and having lost Ellen at this point, I stopped at one particular stand. It was set out simply with a large statue of an angel on the table and a picture hanging on the wall behind it. A lady behind the stand saw me gazing at the picture and told me that it was Angel Ariel. This surprised me, as it wasn't really how I expected an angel might look. I imagined them to be far more beautiful, in fact, much like the one she had on the table in front of her. She told me that she worked with Angel Ariel, channelling messages from the angelic realm. I found this a bit too incredible to believe but, being polite, said nothing of my thoughts.

She then said that there would be a talk in the gallery in thirty minutes' time on Integrated Energy Therapy®, or I.E.T.®, which is used to establish the link to the angelic realm and anyone was welcome to come along. Wandering around the stalls, I couldn't get the image of Ariel out of my mind although I had no idea why. Catching up with Ellen, I asked if she fancied going along to a talk on angels. She looked slightly surprised but agreed and a few minutes later we were climbing the stairs to a small gallery where about 50 people had gathered.

We all sat quietly while the speaker relayed how she had become involved with I.E.T.® and working with angels. She explained that she communicated with angels through the use of 'heartlinks', channelling their energy into this world through an invisible cord. This concept continued to elude me, until we were asked to close our eyes while the speaker channelled angelic energy to us. Everyone obliged, and we carried on listening as she spoke. Suddenly, though my eyes were closed, I began to clearly see an enormous ball of red fire descending on to the top of my head. I couldn't feel its heat, yet instinctively knew that it was intensely hot and very strong. It seemed to be settled over the top of my head the whole time she was talking.

The ability to see another reality clearly while one's eyes are closed is known as seeing with the 'third eye' – though at the time I had no understanding of this term. When we were asked to open our eyes again, I turned to Ellen in amazement, describing what I had seen and felt, asking if she had experienced the same thing – or something like it. Ellen replied that she hadn't seen anything and looked at me as if I had gone slightly mad. As others began to share what they had felt during the exercise, it soon became obvious that no-one else had experienced the same ball of fire. Realising this, I decided not to share it with anyone else … until now.

Being so impressed and slightly overawed by this strange experience, I returned to the stand after the talk. On reaching it, I found a healing was being performed on a woman seated in a chair. Her eyes were closed and she seemed to be totally oblivious to what was going on around her – a fascinating feat given the considerable amount of noise and activity all around.

Above the chair, was a hand-written sign advertising a fifteen-minute healing for €20 and I made an impulsive decision to have one. When the chair was empty, I was invited to be seated and to close my eyes. And so, for the third time since receiving my gift voucher, I obligingly closed my eyes.

Within seconds, I was witness to a scene that played out clearly with my eyes shut, a scene that I will always remember. Whereas earlier there had been colours that seemed to form flames above my head, I now perceived a 'presence'. Though I had never seen one before, I instantly knew it as the angel who had communicated with Sally in the shop, although I am still not able to explain how I knew this.

In the scene I was a child again, of about six or seven years old and the young, beautiful woman was standing before me in a white flowing dress. She was tall and slim, with a cascade of brown hair that draped her shoulders and we stood together on a hillside covered with wild flowers and butterflies. She approached me, saying 'Would you like to play a game?'

Slightly surprised by this question, I asked, 'Which one?'

Smiling at me, she replied, 'We can play whatever game you choose.'

This was unfolding before me while sitting quietly on the same chair where I had seen the other healing take place. Like the woman before me, I was oblivious to the noise and bustle around me. I could clearly hear people talking near the stand, but they just seemed insignificant and to have lost meaning in the here and now. In a way that I couldn't explain or understand, I had moved from the physical world into a spiritual one in the blink of an eye and, incredibly, I felt right at home.

It didn't take long to pick a game since I was so young and we were soon playing 'chase', followed by 'hide and seek'. There was much laughter as we raced and tumbled through the field, heading down towards a river. When we reached it, the young woman didn't pause for a second, running straight across the water without causing a ripple on the surface. I stopped, staring over at her, stunned by what she had just done. Turning back she asked, 'Why didn't you follow me?'

'You are not playing fair! I can't walk across water like you can,' I shouted back across to her.

Laughingly she told me that I could do it and to try. Fear of falling into the water and doing something unknown held me back. I was also acutely aware that I didn't like being separated from her, a fact that seemed to hold huge significance, but I refused to try. Then – seemingly from nowhere, stepping stones appeared in a line across the river. Not hesitating for a moment, I skipped across and was soon by her side once more. Night was beginning to fall, so we lit a campfire together and sat nearby, singing songs from my childhood. Suddenly in the middle of a song she abruptly stood up,

'It's time to leave,' she said.

Within an instant, I was back on the hillside but now standing alone among the flowers and butterflies. At that same moment, I was asked to open my eyes again.

This time, there were no words to describe what I had just witnessed, and I stared up at the lady, speechless. She smiled and asked if the healing had been enjoyable. I immediately knew that once again, no one had shared my experience. Somehow managing to find my tongue, I began to tell her what just occurred. She was amazed and urged me to take part in a course connected with angels she was facilitating.

Later that evening, still slightly bemused, I started sorting through the various leaflets I had accumulated from the festival. I kept a few, including the one about the course with the angels, which was to be held in about six weeks' time. It was a three-day course and seemed quite expensive to me. It was also in a town that was a good three-hour drive away, so I didn't give it much more thought that evening.

A weekend of awakening

Over the next couple of weeks I kept picking the leaflet up. Whenever I sat down for a cup of tea, I would get it out to read again. Eventually, frustrated, I rang Ellen, telling her about the course and asked if she would be interested in going along. She agreed and the following day we posted off our deposits. The next few weeks were then spent frantically saving up the balance, all the while wondering what on earth I was doing.

When the weekend finally arrived, we were really looking forward to a few days away. We arrived early on a Saturday morning along with the group of seven women and two men from various locations around the country. The lady from the stand was also there and introduced herself as Gretta Murphy and the course began.

Gretta explained that the course we were about to embark on was I.E.T.® to the advanced level. We learned that the first thing that needed to be done was for Gretta to attune us to the angelic realm.

She proceeded to do this while we meditated as a group, with our eyes closed. I now know that we were attuned individually to become almost like empty vessels, allowing energy from another realm to flow through us. Through this attunement, each person then became a facilitator in a process of healing, channelling angelic energy to this world. This sounds unbelievable and, to be honest, it did to me at the time too, but as we practised the process of channelling, Ellen and I became aware that something was happening that neither of us really understood or recognised. We could feel an overwhelming sense of peace and calm around us as we worked throughout the weekend.

By the last day, we were thoroughly enjoying the company of our new friends and over lunch, I decided to share the story of my gift voucher. I finished by telling everyone about the mysterious Gretta McCarthy, explaining how we had given up on our search for her as we didn't know where to start looking. At that point, Gretta revealed that her married name was, in fact, McCarthy, but that she liked to be known by her maiden name, Murphy. It is seldom that I am ever at a loss for words, but I was speechless. How had I not noticed her name?

After lunch I went in search of certificates hanging on her walls and sure enough, the name Gretta McCarthy was on each of them. As Gretta was using her maiden name on her leaflets, I had totally overlooked the coincidence of her first name. Yet here I was, faced with the reality that I had found the woman the medium had told me to look for in less than a year. It seemed unbelievable, yet no matter how often I ran the series of events through my stubbornly logical mind, writing it off as a mere coincidence was not possible.

That evening we said our goodbyes, promising to keep in touch as one does and everyone left clutching their certificates to show they had completed the advanced level in I.E.T.®. Our worlds were now opened to the angelic realm and little did I realise what was in store. Quite sure that if I had, I probably would never have gone. I was aware that something quite powerful must have happened if it had had the capability to bring me this far into unknown territory with such ease.

Once home, Lee and Thomas gathered around me to hear about the events of the weekend. I should add that while my sons had a moderately religious upbringing, I would describe myself as neither overly religious nor dismissive of faith. I feel this helped them develop a healthy viewpoint from which they could then decide for themselves how best they wanted to interpret religion. Thinking back on it now though, they must have wondered what on earth had happened to their sensible mother. To their credit, they sat and listened to everything I had to say and even let me give them a heartlink.

Lying in bed that night, mulling over the events of the weekend, for some reason I became extremely agitated at the possibility of being able to see angels with my physical eye, even though I had not been able to up to that point.

Because I am afraid of the dark, the thought that one might appear beside my bed in the middle of the night to speak to me felt no more welcome than the appearance of a ghost. To combat this new-found fear, in the still silence of the night, I said a little prayer asking the angels never to do anything that might startle me. Feeling somewhat reassured by this, I snuggled down and drifted off to sleep. I am not so sure I would have been quite so easily placated if I had had any notion of the sheer volume of angels and spirits that were soon to come into my life at every opportunity and everywhere I went, from that night forward.

2

Struggling to Adapt

*L*ife was hectic working full-time, so it was only in the evenings that heartlink techniques and healings were practised on friends and family. The more I practised the more people seemed to comment on how calm and peaceful they felt, while I too was astonished by the bright colours visible through my third eye as I channelled energy.

Even as my abilities appeared to be developing, I found that there was little time to set aside for this type of energy work and did not pursue it to any great extent. There were other reasons for my reluctance to delve further into the world of healing. My role as a professional involves working with children and I am often entrusted with life-changing decisions shared with other professionals. This is a responsibility that cannot be taken lightly. I felt that if the nature of my new-found ability became known, it might interfere with my career. Having to choose between my job and healings was a prospect I was unwilling to consider at the time.

Also, in our town everyone's affairs are quite well-known. I believed that many people in the community would not be open to my involvement in angelic healings. My sons agreed that it might be best for all concerned to say very little on the matter so I kept it within my close circle of friends and life carried on in this way for a further six months until I heard from Gretta again.

She rang to say that she was giving a day course in I.E.T.® and wondered whether I was interested in attending and bringing the boys along. Unsure what their reaction would be since they were seventeen and nineteen years of age, that evening over dinner I tentatively asked them if they would like to meet Gretta and take part in a workshop. To my surprise they both agreed and the following weekend we set off.

There was a smaller group present for this interactive workshop. Everyone attending was attuned to the angelic energy field and different angels were invited into the room. We were then asked to write down anything we either felt or saw and Lee and Thomas stunned me when they began scribbling frantically in their workbooks. We were invited to share our experiences and they described different angels as they had appeared to them in the room. I did not believe them for a moment and hissed across to stop messing about, but they confessed that they really were seeing these figures and seemed taken aback by the whole experience.

On our return home, occasionally we would sit and send heartlinks together. I felt much more at ease with the whole process now that the boys were also attuned to I.E.T.® and I relaxed into this extraordinary experience with more confidence. We soon became aware that Thomas could see images with his physical eye as clairvoyants do, while Lee had the gift of clairsentience, an amazing ability to sense the emotions of people around him and truths. As for myself, I continued, at first, to see only flashes of vibrant colours through my third eye. But as the months passed, beautiful faces, wings, flowers and animals began to swirl before my closed eyes, until ultimately there appeared to be no limit to what I could see.

Life was running smoothly, until we sensed that a different energy had entered our home. None of us knew what to make of it, but both boys felt the touch of something cold brush across their skin on different occasions. Then one night I was awakened by the feeling of being roughly shaken on the shoulder. As there was no-one else in the room, I could only presume that a spirit could have done this. Lying wide awake in the bed alone, I was petrified.

The following morning I rang Gretta for some advice as to how we could get rid of our unwelcome guest. Gretta told me that I must firmly tell the spirit to leave the house. This sounded too simple to be true, but definitely worth a try. Leaving work that day there was only one task in my mind – to remove the spirit from our house.

On arriving home my immediate dilemma was deciding where best to stand to clear a spirit, as I had not thought to ask Gretta about that. Sighing heavily, I glanced around the house trying to decide what to do next. The original house has been extended on both sides – one side incorporating the living quarters of previous farm labourers and on the other side the stables, but all of them built in different eras. My problem was further exacerbated by the fact that I had no idea which century the spirit belonged to and therefore which building. I decided to position myself next to the old fireplace in our middle room, as this seemed to be the most central point in the house.

Feeling completely ridiculous and clearing my throat loudly, I firmly told the spirit to leave the house. Standing in the ensuing silence, a familiar tingling began to run through my body in strong waves. It was identical to what I had experienced with Sally in the shop when I had first taken hold of her hand. This meant that not only was the spirit still present, but that it was now standing very close to me. Obviously something had gone horribly wrong, although I wasn't really surprised and I was totally at a loss as to what to do next.

Thomas, unbeknownst to me, had been home throughout this ordeal silently doing his homework in the next room. When I went in and saw him there, I threw myself onto the settee beside him and told him what I had been trying to do, just in case he thought I might be going mad. Realising how upset I was, he put down his pen and offered to assist. Given his ability to 'see' with his physical eye, he suggested that we switch off the lights to help him locate the spirit. Rather nervously I agreed to this, as the prospect of searching for a spirit in the dark was not very high on my wish list.

When the lights were out, the quiet of the room seemed strangely deafening and I waited nervously for him to speak. After several long minutes, he said he could see the light of a spirit in the room, which seemed to be trying to avoid his attention. We spent the better part of an hour attempting to locate the spirit as it moved from room to room in an attempt to escape his gaze. It crossed my mind that the spirit might be enjoying itself, but I certainly wasn't, as I tripped and fumbled my way around the house which now seemed so unfamiliar in the pitch black. Eventually, we found ourselves in my bedroom where the spirit had lodged itself inside a corner cupboard. Suddenly losing patience with our futile attempts, I told Thomas that I was going to see if some assistance could be sought from the angelic realm. So, still standing in the eerie darkness, I closed my eyes and sent a heartlink.

Very clearly, through my third eye, I began to see a beautiful indigo-blue mist forming in the dark room. As it grew denser, I became somewhat alarmed when I realised that it was beginning to take the shape of a man standing directly in front of Thomas. Astonished, I turned to where he stood, telling him what I could see. He responded that he already knew what was happening, as he too could see the man and that the man was looking directly at him.

While frantically trying not to be afraid of the darkness, a spirit lodged in my bedroom cupboard and now the sight of a glowing man standing before us, simultaneously we received a telepathic message not to be afraid of the figure as it was Archangel Michael, although I am not sure where the message came from. This was the first time we saw an angel together, Thomas, with his physical eye, and myself, through my third eye. There was no exchange of words with Archangel Michael, other than being told his name. The spirit whom we had been chasing all evening and then forgot about with the appearance of Archangel Michael, never actually left that night. In fact it remained with us for a long time, but that is the story of Jake, and Jake's tale is for another day.

Problems with my family

While we continued desperately trying to understand what was happening to us, others did not. My own family found it hard to grasp what the boys and I could do. This was not hard to understand, as we were struggling with it ourselves. My parents discouraged me from continuing because of the tension it was causing, which was also understandable. Yet, as others have discovered before me, once these types of abilities have surfaced, there is no going back. All this led to an unspoken rift within our family on the subject. As a result, I stopped talking about it, since this seemed to be the only way to resolve the matter. These problems soon made me reluctant to speak openly on the subject of angels with anyone, unless they mentioned them first.

Problems at work

Alongside family dilemmas, it was also an increasing issue dealing with this ability while at work. I had already tried to address this problem by not practising healing work of any kind, but I had not considered the perception of children.

One afternoon while working with a six-year-old girl, she casually mentioned that her mother was standing behind me in her wedding dress. This statement rattled me to the bone, as the child's mother had died the previous year. Doing my best to remain calm, I asked how her mother looked. She replied that her mother looked beautiful and very happy. The spirit had no doubt come down to visit her daughter, taking the chance to use me as a channel. So, while I found that this type of unexpected incident could bring happiness to an individual child, I concluded that, for now, they were best not mentioned to my colleagues in the workplace!

Understanding my role

Incidents such as these made me realise that I was unconsciously attracting spirits as well as angels into my energy field everywhere I went. In a desperate attempt to turn my back on this chapter of my life, I decided to take a career break and return to university for a two-year master's degree. More than anything I longed to be like everyone else again and I desperately wanted my old life back. I continued heartlinking with only my immediate family or close friends, and relative peace and quiet returned to our lives. It seemed that we had been left alone to our own devices.

Of course, I should have known better than to expect such a strong energetic force to be thwarted by any attempt to hide behind a human experience such as this. However, even now, I am glad I did turn away for a while, being totally unprepared for the changes that were occurring in our lives. At the time it felt unfair to be thrown into a world that none of us could understand. Looking back I often wondered if celestial beings watched with some bemusement as we attempted to return to a life without them; a prospect that feels unimaginable now. The day I handed in my last piece of work to the university, angelic beings and spirits moved swiftly back into my life, whether I wanted them there or not. This time, their presence was much more persistent and impossible to ignore.

3

Spirit Encounters

As I grew accustomed to the various vibrations of energy from other realms, I realised that there are subtle differences between the energy of a spirit that is still attached to this world and that of a spirit who is at peace. Then again there is another very clear distinction between these and that of an angelic being. While I am unable to physically feel angelic energy, a spirit can be distinctly chilling when it is nearby or when, as I have on occasion, walked straight through it. Also unlike angelic energy, which is always vividly colourful, spirit energy is more often than not monochromatic.

A spirit who is still present among us does not need to be contacted through the process of channelling. Their energy is very clear to see through my third eye, though there are many people who are unaware of their existence. Spirits that have moved into the next realm only appear for a specific purpose and for a short length of time, usually to pass on a specific message to a loved one. Whatever sort of spirit is near me, a tingling sensation rushes through my body once I am aware of their presence. When I acknowledge them, this tingling can become quite strong and overwhelming, similar to the first time it occurred in the shop with the medium. Whereas then the sensation had been alarming, over time I have grown used to this process of communication.

Often, it is immediately obvious to me when there is a spirit present in someone's home, but, to be honest, if I tried to make contact with each one that I ever came across, I would never get anything done. Also, I rarely try to contact spirits unless absolutely necessary. This could very well be because so many attempt to make contact with me, even at very awkward moments, that it would be ludicrous to go in search of them.

People often ask if there are spirits or angels in their homes or standing beside them. I am aware that many get great comfort by the thought of a deceased loved one or an angel being close to them. But spirits, in a similar way to angels, can be very discreet and also sometimes very individual to that particular person. Therefore I feel no compulsion to attempt to make contact with one simply because someone has asked me to. Angels and spirits can be quite content simply watching over us and, because of this, I would generally answer these questions rather vaguely, whether I am aware of a presence or not.

Channelling messages from spirits

It didn't take long to learn that it is very easy to talk to a spirit. The first time this happened I was totally unprepared for it. I was at my parents' house and dad had agreed to have a heartlink. As you are already aware, my family is not particularly open to my healing work and I was surprised that dad agreed to have one at all.

We sat close together in the living room and the angels were invited in. They were delighted to be able to reach my father and there was a lot of activity around him. Suddenly a different energy began to channel through at the same time as the angels. I didn't recognise it at first, but just knew that it was different from angelic energy. Sitting in silence beside my father, I tried to gauge the situation as I didn't want anything to go wrong when he was involved.

As the presence strengthened, it became recognisable as that of a spirit who had taken the opportunity to reach my father. Telepathically I was told the spirit's name was Thomas and that he was my father's dad – my grandad. Grandad asked me to tell my father that he was very proud of him and that he was sorry that he had not gone to watch him play football on Saturdays. I agreed and he soon left. Shortly after, the angels also left the room and we were once again left sitting alone.

This was the first time a spirit had given me not only a name but also a clear message to pass on. Glancing nervously at dad who was still sitting quietly beside me, it was hard to decide what to do. It had been a huge step forward for him to accept a heartlink, but it was quite another matter to receive a message from his dad who had passed away many years ago. Frustrated by the situation in which I had been placed I knew something had to be said.

'Was your dad's name Thomas?' I asked Dad hesitantly, I wasn't sure as I'd always only known him as Grandad.

'Yes,' he replied.

Another long pause followed. Then deciding to put my fate in the hands of the gods, I relayed the clear message that I had just received and then waited anxiously for his reaction. Surprisingly, he took it very well, telling me all about his youth. He explained that while he had always played 'footie' on Saturdays, his dad had rarely gone to watch. Another long silence followed, until rather nervously I asked,

'Have I upset you, Dad?'

'No,' he replied. 'Thank you.'

Of all my channelling experiences, this has remained so special to me. I had been very fond of my grandad and it was lovely to have been able to help him communicate directly with his only son. Since this time, my grandad's presence has often appeared beside me, alongside many other spirits and from these interactions I have many other interesting stories to relate.

Jake

The spirit of Jake became rather special too. This could possibly be because he is the first spirit with whom I took the brave step of actually speaking to, or it could simply be because he lived with us.

A few months after the incident when Thomas and I saw Archangel Michael in my bedroom, Gretta rang to invite me to another workshop. This time I went alone. The specifics of the day are rather vague, but I do recall talking to another woman over lunch. As we chatted, she told me that she could feel a spirit's presence all around me. She told me that although she had never seen my home, she felt that the spirit was of a man who stands by our fireplace in our middle room. She suggested that his energy should be cleared from the house straight away. This information gave me the creeps.

On returning home I decided to try and clear away the spirit using the same technique I had already tried, albeit unsuccessfully, by simply asking it to leave. Over the preceding months I had become much more confident in my approach to spirits. My fear had been replaced by exasperation, simply by the sheer number that seemed to follow me everywhere I went. This time I felt reasonably confident of success.

Both sons were home, so I told them what I was about to do. Thomas stopped me and asked why I never tried to make contact with a spirit to find out why it was still there. He felt it was wrong to clear the energy of a spirit away without first asking why it had remained. Slightly taken aback by his point of view, I argued that chatting to spirits wasn't too high on my list of priorities, but he persisted. Therefore, later that evening, for the first time

I nervously began a conversation with a spirit by asking its name and I soon found myself deep in conversation with an old man called Jake.

It appears that Jake worked as a labourer on the farm that is now our home in or around the 1820s. He appeared to be a mild-mannered man, very much reminding me of my father. For some reason he wanted me to be made aware of his old worn hands. Forgetting that we were now chatting across different parallels, I explained as simply as I could, that it was time for him to leave as he had in fact, died many years ago and that there was no reason for him to stay anymore.

He replied by asking if he could stay, as he was happy watching over us. I was so taken aback by this request that I wasn't sure what to do next. I went in search of the boys for advice. They both agreed that they saw no reason why Jake should not stay and so, for a good number of years, his gentle presence remained with us.

This presence did not go unnoticed. The first person to comment on it was my boss. She had called to the house one evening to drop off some paperwork and went upstairs to use the bathroom. On returning downstairs she asked, 'Do you know there is a spirit of a man standing at the top of your stairs?'

I don't know who was more startled by this revelation: my boss, by what she had just seen, or myself, that she was able to see it. As we stared at each other in silence, both unsure of what to do or say next, I at last answered, 'Err-well yes, actually we do know. It's Jake. He's quite harmless though.'

To this day I don't think there are many occasions when this incident has not come up as a party piece when we are both in company and, thankfully, I still have my job.

Jake was also seen by my friend Ann, who lives in England. She is a close friend of the whole family and visits us every year. She is also psychic. We had always known that she was aware of spirits and while this had fascinated us to some extent, it had never been something we had dwelt on, or considered to be something we wanted to know more about, until our own lives changed so much. We listened patiently to her stories, making appropriate comments as she relayed her tales, but now that I was communicating with angels and spirits, she had become my greatest ally. When she came to stay, I'm afraid she was quizzed endlessly about her own abilities and also asked if she had any idea what was happening to us.

It was not too long before Ann and Jake 'bumped' into each other. She had previously admitted that she was quite nervous in our house at night, as she was aware of an exceptional amount of energy everywhere, insisting on a light being left on in her bedroom. Unfortunately, Jake thought that night-time was as good a time as any to introduce himself to Ann and, standing close to her bed, woke her up. Ann recounted to us all what happened next. She said that when she awoke, a tallish man in a dark overcoat was standing beside the bed watching her and to put it mildly, she was terrified.

To overcome her fear, she spoke to him firmly, 'What are you doing here?'

Jake's retort was immediate. 'What are YOU doing here?'

Slightly nonplussed by this reply, she firmly asked him to go away – which he did, until an hour later when he woke her again!

Other people also mentioned Jake, or rather the fact that they are aware of a 'presence' in the house. On two separate occasions, friends commented on a feeling of being watched as they went about our house. Knowing exactly who was 'watching' them, I asked if it bothered them. They both replied no, except that it made them feel slightly nervous, especially if it was starting to get dark. Apologising profusely to them, I took care not to relay their stories to each other as I was beginning to get worried that I might start losing my friends! Later that evening, Jake was told in no uncertain terms that if he wanted to remain, he was going to have to be much more discreet or he would have to leave. Setting this boundary seemed to establish a relationship that appeared to work well for all of us, as the last time he was seen, he had been happily pushing a wheelbarrow across the back garden. Not long after this, his presence left the house. I never knew why or how, but one morning I woke up and realised that he had gone.

Although Jake had been left to his own devices, albeit with some restrictions, it would be very rare that I would do this once I have made contact with a spirit. Their energy can be very draining for the people living in the same house. This became apparent simply because once a spirit has been guided to their appropriate realm, the difference in a house's energy can be quite incredible. Even people who would usually sense very little, comment on this change. The simplest way it could be described is as a 'lightness'. I remember this feeling distinctly in a house that we visited to try to 'clear' as a family.

Our first and last 'house clearing' as a family

A friend of mine had told me, on many occasions, that one of her sons was constantly waking at night, saying that there were monsters on his bed. She and her husband always tried to reassure him that everything was alright, but it was happening so often that she began to wonder if there really was something sinister in the house. I asked if she would like me to come over to see if there was anything out of the ordinary happening. She was delighted with the offer. Since she was a close friend of the family she was aware of the boys' abilities and so the spiritual trident that was our little family went along to her house.

We chose a time when we knew everybody would be out and found our way to the children's bedroom. We all instantly picked up a sinister energy lurking in the room. Thomas said he could see that something was crouched down on the lower bunk bed where my friend had said that the boy slept. Turning to Lee I asked if he could pick up any past emotions lingering in the room, but was alarmed to see that he was doubled over and in a very distressed state. Being clairsentient meant that as well as knowing 'truths', he is able to sense sorrow and grieving associated with death, thus experiencing a plethora of emotions and sensations that can occur when events are recalled from the past. No words were needed to know that he had become attuned to a very negative vibration. Because of his obvious distress we immediately told him to leave the house. The two of us remained to quickly establish what had happened here, so that we too could go.

Opening ourselves up to the spirit world, we became aware of a large gathering of women and children who appeared to have been trapped in this area. I say 'area' as I could sense that whenever these people had been in the room, the building was not as it looked now, with room sizes and shapes being different. This seemed obvious as some of the people appeared to be inside walls. Buildings that look nothing like they are now is a common occurrence when entering the past through telepathy. Because of this, I usually avoid being upstairs when entering the past! I have no idea what happened to these people or why, but did know that I had no intention of hanging around to find out. Having the intelligence not to delve into a situation that may not only disturb my own energy, but also keep me awake for weeks. We quickly called in the angels to help us clear the room, waiting until the energy quietened and then became still.

We were soon making our way back down the stairs, when we both sensed another presence in the house. After a quick discussion, we decided that it seemed pointless leaving if there was another spirit somewhere else, so we started checking all the rooms. The last room we entered was the living room and Thomas immediately noticed a male spirit standing behind the television in a corner of the room.

Not wanting to linger, we quickly spoke to him through telepathy, asking why he was here. He told us that he was waiting for his wife. He explained that she had gone out to collect wood and hadn't yet returned. Looking at him closely it appeared that he was from around the eighteenth century and had therefore been waiting a long time. I tried explaining to him, as well as one can, that his wife would not be returning, as she had actually been dead for many years and that he needed to leave now too in order to see her again.

While this might sound simplistic, these situations can be anything but, and this occasion proved to be no different. He had no intention of leaving until she came home and we all stood facing each other across the room. Not sure what to do next, suddenly I had an idea. Sending up a heartlink, I asked if there was any possibility of this man's wife being found so that she could make contact with him. Feeling slightly ridiculous I turned to Thomas telling him of my request. He shrugged his shoulders saying it was worth a try. After waiting a few minutes in complete silence, we began to notice that the energy of the room was changing in a way neither of us recognised and as we watched, one of the most incredible things I have ever witnessed happened. His wife's energy began to descend into the middle of the room before us. Who could have believed such a thing was possible? Immediately, there was movement from behind the television and the man went across to her. The intensity of the emotions that followed were indescribable as the couple were reunited. When she turned to return from where she had come, there was no hesitation on his part and as he followed her, the lightness we associate with the exit of a spirit filled the room.

Saying goodbye to Uncle Denis

As a family, we have always acknowledged the importance of finding the time to say goodbye properly. For example, no matter where we are, when parting company we always give each other a hug and a kiss. It almost seemed like second nature until the day when Lee, then twelve years old, said something as I was leaving the house. As he was seeing me out, he told me that it was always important to say goodbye properly, as you never knew if you would see that person again. Impressed by such words of wisdom from one so young, it brought back memories of a time when the chance to say goodbye was stolen from me by the untimely death of Uncle Denis. It also made me wonder if unconsciously, I had implemented this habit into my family because of that experience.

Uncle Denis was one of my mother's nine brothers and although they were all really nice, he was my favourite. Even at a young age I knew he was fond of me too, and as he played his guitar he would often wink over at me, making me giggle. He was married to my Auntie Barbara and they were very much in love. Unfortunately they were never able to have children of their own, thus making it easy for them to spoil us rotten. They spent a lot of time with my family as we grew up, even coming on our annual summer holidays to Wales. No family event seemed complete without them, including my wedding and the christening of my first son.

When I was seven months pregnant with my second son, Mum began saying that Uncle Denis seemed to be suffering from a lot of headaches. They had moved to the south of England a year earlier and we didn't see as much of them as we used to. In fact we hardly saw them at all. I took in what mum was saying, but didn't pay much heed, probably because I was busy with a toddler and struggling, being heavily pregnant in the middle of an exceptionally hot summer. A month later Denis was admitted to hospital.

This was a particularly upsetting time for the family, as everyone began travelling to see him, although no-one wanted to take me on the twelve-hour round trip because of my condition. While I was unhappy with this arrangement, it didn't seem to be something to argue about as everyone was so distressed and it was obvious something was very wrong. After a few weeks Uncle Denis was allowed home, bringing much needed hope for everyone. I planned to visit him after the birth of my baby and life went on as usual for a few more weeks.

I was just thinking of writing to my uncle telling him of my plans, when my contractions began and Thomas was born. Therefore the letter was never written and two days later Uncle Denis died.

I was devastated. Not only had I missed the chance to see him while he was ill, but the chance to say goodbye had gone forever. How could this have happened? No-one could stop me attending his funeral with my new baby even though everyone advised me against it as I had only just left hospital. My loss, and that of everyone else, was enormous. How could such a lovely person be so cruelly taken at such a young age?

Life continued as it does, and for us it was without Uncle Denis. This was a long time before the gift voucher was ever placed in my hand or the ability to communicate with spirits began, yet somehow I began to sense his presence near me. It is impossible to explain this awareness, other than to say that there was no denying it was him. At first, it happened occasionally, while out in the fields playing with my sons or when pushing the pram, but over time I grew to realise that he was with me almost constantly. His presence became so much a part of my life that it became easy to forget he was there. Amazed by this sensation, I mentioned it to my mum but she hastily told me it would be best to keep it to myself, as my auntie was not coping well with the loss of her husband. Mum was right and Auntie Barbara died a few short years later, also at a young age. As we all huddled together around another coffin, although no-one said as much, there was no doubt in anyone's mind, that she had gone to be reunited with him once again.

Not long after the I.E.T.® course all those years later, while sitting down with Lee and Thomas one evening practising heartlinks, we noticed the energy of the room changing and when it settled, to my astonishment, before us stood Uncle Denis. He was dressed exactly as I remembered him and after staring at him for a minute in stunned disbelief I burst out crying. The boys stood up and left the room telling me later that they were asked to leave.

The next half hour was spent in the company of Uncle Denis. First and foremost was the need to apologise for not visiting him when he was so ill and also not taking the time to write the letter. It was not until doing this that I realised how much of a burden the guilt of this had been for me. After that, through my mind, we visited all of the times we had shared together. He gave me as much time as was needed to do this and was as patient and kind as ever. When my memory bank was exhausted, we stayed together awhile, until eventually I asked,

'Will I ever see you again?'

'I don't know,' he replied, 'but I am never far away,' and with that he left.

While this experience was unexpected, it helped me

significantly in the process of letting him go. After he had gone, I sat pondering about all the other people that must be in a similar position. Consumed with guilt because of something they did or didn't do or say to someone who passed over before the situation can be resolved and my heart went out to them. I now recognised the feeling of heaviness that had been weighing on my own heart because I did not get a chance to say goodbye and thank Uncle Denis for all the good times we had together. So now when leaving the house, I always find the time for that last hug or kiss and remember my son and his wise words of wisdom.

Ignoring a spirit

Moving on to a lighter note, I thought to share one funny tale with you of a time when ignoring a spirit's wish to communicate resulted in chaos.

Our house is very old and could probably write a few books of its own and, luckily, some of these stories have been relayed to me in quite unexpected ways. Since we moved here, three different families have come knocking on the door to ask if they could come in to see the house. They had all either been born in it, grown up in it or had happy memories of the place. One such visitor came all the way from America.

Answering a knock at the door one summer's morning, I found a young couple before me. Apologising profusely for disturbing us, they asked if it would be possible for their grandmother, who was visiting from the States, to come inside and see where she had been born, one last time. Without hesitation they were all invited in and they went back to the car to get her.

This lady was well into her eighties and there was no doubt that she had come to say farewell to her homeland for the last time. They were a lovely family and we were all soon chatting over a cup of tea as she pottered about. After a while she decided that she wanted to see the room where she had been born. Since this was upstairs it posed some problems as she was quite frail. After much debate we managed to get her up the steep stairs and along the hallway to her place of birth, leaving her there alone with her memories.

On my way back down the stairs I became aware of the presence of a spirit. I was enjoying chatting to the other family members and therefore tried to ignore it. But the tingling throughout my body suddenly became very strong, so strong in fact, that it nearly took my breath away. Trying to smile sweetly at my unexpected visitors, as I poured out yet more tea, telepathically I communicated with the spirit asking what was so urgent that we needed to chat right now – and couldn't it see it was an incredibly inconvenient time? The spirit replied by saying that she was the old woman's mother and would I tell her daughter that she was here with her. While this was without doubt an incredibly touching moment, it seemed totally impractical and I told her as much. In fact, we almost began to have a telepathic argument. She refused to leave until I said something and I refused to do it. The poor old lady upstairs had travelled thousands of miles to say her goodbyes in Ireland and I certainly wasn't going to bring up the fact that I had a very unusual ability to communicate with spirits, and that by some amazing coincidence, was speaking with her mother right now. Could you imagine what response would be forthcoming from total strangers? I thought the spirit was being particularly unfair.

In the meantime, the old lady was attempting to come back down the stairs and we all rushed forward to help. The spirit lost patience with me at this stage and set off all our smoke alarms. We have become used to this ploy used by spirits to gain our attention over the years, but this was our first experience of this kind of behaviour. As the spirit tried this last desperate attempt to get her daughter's attention, my sons went around trying to disconnect the batteries, but seemed to be having some difficulty. I tried to hurry the family out of the house as politely as possible so that some sort of calm could be restored to our home.

Falling into the nearest chair with relief when they finally left to the chorus of alarms, I told the boys what had happened. They agreed that it had been the right thing to do in saying nothing. Nevertheless, this experience has played on my mind many a time since. It forced me to acknowledge the frustration and dilemma spirits must feel when they can't communicate with loved ones. I hope that if the mother and daughter are together once more as

I do believe they are, that they forgive me.

Carrots and potatoes

A few years ago we decided to knock down a building on our land that had been derelict for a long time, as it had become unstable and dangerous. It took quite some time to come to terms with the fact that it had to go. I have always had a fascination with old buildings, whether derelict or not, and have often felt that each is unique in its own way. Whatever state they may now be in, they had once been homes, built by local workmen using stones dug from small quarries. Many of these houses were grouped together in small hamlets, forming tight-knit communities and examples of these can still be seen dotted across the Irish countryside. They never fail to catch my imagination, as I try to imagine how life must once have been. Often perched precariously on steep hillsides overlooking the Atlantic sea, one wonders how anyone survived in the depth of winter at all. Many miles from the nearest town or village, some are so remote, that 'church' was sometimes a large stone set a field, from which the local priest would say mass.

Now these houses are empty and the altars serve only as tourist attractions. Many buildings have fallen into disrepair just like ours, providing only shelter for many species of wildlife. While these inhabitants may not be the intended ones, they still breathe life into otherwise silent spaces. Wandering among these windowless, and more often than not roofless, buildings trying to picture the past, I never imagined for one moment that there was a possibility of being watched by spirits hundreds of years old, locked within their stories. Therefore, while the demolition of our building caused me a certain amount of reflection and concern for the birds nesting inside it, it evoked a different reaction from one particular spirit: that of outrage.

A few days after the building had been taken down we all worked outside, picking through the old stones to salvage some of the better ones to rebuild a wall. After a few hours it was time to make some lunch and I went back inside to wash my hands, making my way along the hallway to the bathroom. As I did, I distinctly felt the presence of a spirit but tried to ignore it. While washing my hands the hair on the back of my neck began to stand on end and the tingling sensation, signalling a spirit was nearby, swept through my whole body. Feeling slightly nervous and very much alone, I continued washing my hands. I then dried them slowly on the towel, all the while dreading the moment when I had to turn round. Mentally asking for some protection from the angels, I swung around to face whoever was there with as much courage as one can muster in these circumstances.

In the corner of the room, clearly visible through my third eye, was a small old woman dressed in black. For one moment I was slightly amused, as she appeared to be standing in the bath, but this amusement was short lived. She was furious. The force of her fury hit me like a wave, and it was stronger and deeper than any feeling of anger I had encountered in my life. Not waiting for me to communicate first, she told me that she was incensed that her house had been knocked down and how dare we do that to her home. Slightly thrown off guard by the reason for her anger, there was a moment's silence. Exploring her energy it was obvious that she was from around the nineteenth century, probably the 1880s. I decided to ask her why she had stayed within this realm for so long, but now, after venting her anger, she was refusing to speak to me and had half turned away. I was quite fascinated by the fact that now that her home had been demolished, she was able to move into another house so quickly. At the same time I knew that she could not stay here either.

As diplomatically as possible, I told her that she had died many years ago and now needed to leave to be once more with her loved ones, and that this was possible with my help. There was a pause while she considered this information, although her reluctance to speak with me was obvious. She then told me she would leave on the oath of a promise. She said the reason she couldn't rest was because she was worried that her family would starve to death without her, as they were very poor. Therefore the promise was that I would plant potatoes and carrots every year so that she could rest in peace, safe in the knowledge that food was always available. Just stopping myself from groaning out loud, the deal was reached, as growing vegetables of any description is not one of my strong points. Flowers, herbs and fruit respond to my every touch, but vegetables were another matter entirely, as I battle to keep them not only alive, but more importantly uneaten by the various wildlife that visits my plot. Once this deal was struck it was quite surprising how quickly she left and I wondered rather guiltily if this was simply because she no longer had anywhere to call home.

Living dangerously

Some friends of ours own a house surrounded by a number of old stone cottages, outhouses and stables, in varying states of repair. It wouldn't be hard to imagine that at one time this property was quite a large, prosperous farm. Pottering about inside these buildings is like taking a step back in time as they are full of relics from the past, including letters dating as far back as the 1880s, hand-written shop receipts, coins and general memorabilia, all of which fascinate me enormously. One day Ellen came to visit my friend too, as she had never been before.

After the customary cup of tea we all went outside to look at an impressive collection of buildings. Once we were inside what must have been the main house, Ellen, being a chef, made a beeline for the fireplace and the various cooking implements hanging on the walls. Not being in the slightest bit interested in cooking, I left my friends chatting, while I wandered off into the next room. This room was much smaller than the main one, possibly being a bedroom and one I had never been in before. Glancing around, I became aware of energy that seemed

43

to be lingering in the room. Since there was no-one with me, I tried to access the energy more clearly with my third eye. I had an image of people sitting down to dinner in the next room and there seemed to be a large family present at the meal, with many daughters. They appeared to be very happy, and the importance of the father as the head of the family was obvious. However, it wasn't the family scene in the next room that caught my attention but something in the room where I was now standing. Knowing that either of my two friends could disturb my concentration at any moment, I decided to rejoin them in the main room.

Later that evening while in bed, intrigued by what I had seen, I tried to bring the scene from the house back into my mind. And, feeling much more relaxed, with no one to disturb me, within seconds the scene was once more played out before me and a very interesting story began to unfold.

It began with the family sitting down to dinner and although their happiness as a family unit was apparent, there was a tension in the air that was now tangible. Scanning the room to try and establish what was causing it was slightly confusing. Nothing apparently was wrong. Not content, I decided to tap into the bedroom where I had stood earlier while my friends had chatted about the ancient fireplace. Straight away, I picked up on the presence of a boy of about fourteen years of age who was not a member of the family. Fascinated, a secret story was played out before me.

It appeared that the boy was on some sort of mission, carrying an important message from one town to another, by foot at night. This house was situated near the main road he was travelling along and the family were harbouring him during the day so he could rest before continuing on his journey through the next night. The message he carried was of great importance to the local community, but was also a closely guarded secret and many lives depended on his whereabouts remaining secret. Beginning to get caught up in the story, I became somewhat alarmed, not only for the boy, but also for the family. They were evidently putting themselves in great danger hiding the child, as the police were aware that something was afoot.

The intriguing twist of this tale was that the local police would not call to the house as the General was deeply in love with one of the daughters and did not wish to upset her father. He appeared to be a well-respected man, not only by his community but also by the authorities and would not be suspected of being involved in anything underhand.

Astonished by the scene, I had no idea as to why the energy had remained in the house for so long, thinking perhaps that the tale had a gruesome end, half-afraid to watch it any further. Thankfully the boy slipped away under the cover of darkness of the night and the rest of his journey was completed safely, while the family also remaining unharmed. What the message was about, or for whom it was intended, was not revealed. Perhaps it was in connection with some form of uprising against the authorities of the time, so unfortunately there is no end for this tale except to say that thankfully, everyone survived.

4

Love, Oh What Tangled Webs We Weave

The cottage by the sea

$\mathcal{A}$ few years ago, Lee and his partner, Anne, decided to move out of an apartment they had been renting in town to move into a cottage by the sea. They were expecting their first child and one day while travelling in their area, I decided to call in. Delighted to find them home we were soon chatting over a cup of tea about the imminent birth and the new house. Anne said everything was going well except that neither of them were sleeping very well. They didn't know why this should be as they were both working full time and were consequently tired each evening.

Before leaving, I needed to use the bathroom. On the small landing at the top of the stairs there was a distinct change in room temperature. It was freezing, a temperature instantly recognisable as that of a spirit's presence. Returning downstairs, we said our farewells and I left without mentioning the presence of a spirit.

A few weeks later I decided to visit again. This time only Lee was home and he soon brought up the subject of how badly they were sleeping. He said that it was now so bad, that Anne was becoming distressed about it but they couldn't imagine what was wrong. Knowing exactly what was the problem, I decided something needed to be said. Aware of how sensitive he was to negative energy, I tentatively suggested that perhaps there may be some unsettling energy from the past within the house that needed clearing. He thought about this for a moment, before saying that as long as we didn't tell Anne, he would be delighted if I could help as she was becoming so upset at night that something needed to be done. More than happy to oblige, I agreed to this and went upstairs alone.

A tale unfolds

At the top of the stairs, I wasn't feeling quite so brave and, feeling rather vulnerable on my own, I nervously allowed myself to open up to the spirit world. It didn't take long for something to happen and I soon found that I was standing in a large room filled with people. The room was totally different to how the house looked now and it took me a few moments to realise that I was actually standing in an entirely different house. It reminded me of pictures of tenement houses I had seen from around the 1800s.

Once I had my bearings, I began to sense intense emotions from the people around me. There were so many that it took a few minutes to associate each one with the person to whom it belonged. The strongest emotion I could feel was one of injustice, palpable from a young sailor who had just returned from sea and it was from him that the tale began to unfold.

A baby had recently been born in the bedroom; in fact the young woman was still in bed holding the infant. There were different generations of one family present in the room with her, but it was the young sailor and the husband of the woman who held my attention. It was unclear if these men were related, but there must have been some connection for them both to be there and I had a feeling they were brothers, but I couldn't be sure. An unspoken tension was building up between them and I sensed it involved the real identity of the father of the newborn baby. Suddenly a fight broke out between them that spilled out onto the landing where I stood and I actually moved back as they passed by me. In the scuffle, the sailor lost his footing and with a cry, fell down the stairs. A deafening silence followed, which seemed to last an eternity, until everyone rushed forward as one, to see what had happened. I too peered down the stairs with the family members to see how he was. But he had landed awkwardly and it was obvious to all, that he was dead.

Pandemonium broke out all around me. I watched, horrified. There were people moving in every direction and the women began wailing, yet my attention was drawn back to the young woman in the bed. She was devastated by what had just taken place and was trying not to show it, yet her grief could be felt keenly. In that instant, I knew that not only had she just lost the love of her life, but also the father of the baby.

The family were in turmoil.

They did not want to report the death as they knew their son might be charged with manslaughter and imprisoned, or even worse.

After much deliberation, they decided to wait until nightfall when, in the stillness of the night, they could take the young man's body from the house to bury him close to a church graveyard that I actually know quite well. They all agreed that if anyone asked about his whereabouts, they would say they hadn't seen him for a long time, and that he had never returned from sea.

I was given the ability to see these events unfold because of the young sailor. He wanted someone to know the truth of what had happened that day. No one ever found out about his death and his spirit could not rest until he had told his story, which he had now managed to do, two hundred years later.

I was deeply saddened by what had taken place in the house. My heart went out, not only to the sailor and the young woman who was trying so hard to hide her grief; but also to all the family members who had been suddenly thrust into the middle of a waking nightmare.

What can you say?

I waited for the energy in the house to settle, until a
familiar feeling of lightness descended upon the house as
the spirit of the sailor left, this time hopefully to join his
loved one at last. His story was told and he was now more
than happy to move on to the next world. I, on the other
hand, was still very much in this world and suddenly
remembered my son downstairs waiting patiently for my
return. I was faced with a dilemma. How could this tale
possibly be recounted without the possibility of him
packing their bags and leaving the house immediately? I
knew how sensitive he would be to the energy of the story
if it was told and it may upset him a great deal. Turning to
the angels I decided to ask for their help. So far they have
never let me down and I very much hoped this occasion
would be no different. Returning downstairs, I found him
waiting patiently with yet another cup of tea and suddenly
it seemed right to tell him the truth. I knew he wouldn't
be happy with anything else. He took it very well and
when the whole tale had been told, he asked how the
house felt now. Relieved, I told him that the energy from
the incident seemed to have cleared, but that we wouldn't
know for sure until they went to bed that night. Agreeing
that I should visit the following week, we gave each other
a hug and said our goodbyes.

As promised, I returned the following week and found
them both at home looking very well. Anne soon got
around to the topic of sleeping. She said that they were

feeling much happier in their new home. She also said how strange it was that they hadn't been able to settle at night, but were now sleeping soundly, laughingly commenting on how the house even felt warmer. Delighted with this news and sharing a knowing look with Lee, nothing was said. My role in this incident was finished, or so I thought.

Later that night in bed, I was suddenly awakened from my sleep. I lay still for a moment, wondering if someone was out of bed, but the house was silent. In the stillness I became aware of energy within the room and by using my third eye could clearly see a group of people circled around my bed. Before there was any time to panic, they communicated with me. They told me that they were the family members who had been present the day of the killing. I was soon wide awake, unnerved by the presence of so many spirits close to me.

For one crazy moment I thought they may have come to kill me, since I now knew the truth. Trying to stay calm, while wildly wondering if spirits could actually do this, I bravely asked them what they wanted. They said that they had come to ask for forgiveness. They said that the guilt of that day had been an unbearable burden on the whole family for the rest of their lives. They needed release from the weight of the guilt by asking someone for forgiveness, as they had been unable to seek absolution from the local priest. They didn't stay long and soon left of their own accord as one. Turning over to go back to sleep, I thought that this sorry story had at last been put to bed after so many years. I couldn't have been more wrong.

The birth of Nathan

Four weeks later Anne gave birth to a beautiful baby boy who they called Nathan. I visited them while they were still in the hospital and promised to call as soon as they were home.

It must have been about a week before I finally stopped by. They had settled into their new way of life as a family and seemed very happy. While Anne was feeding Nathan upstairs, Lee asked me into the kitchen for a cup of tea. Once inside, he closed the door. In a hushed voice he told me they were having difficulty getting Nathan to sleep at all at night, even though they had seen to all his needs. He seemed worried that something was wrong with the house again. It was impossible to check around upstairs as Anne was home, but I promised to try to do something.

Later that night in bed, telepathically I attempted to communicate with any spirit that was still present in the house. Instantly, the spirit of the young woman who had been in the bed holding her new born child all those years ago was beside me. I asked why she was still there. She replied that the presence of Nathan in the room where she had given birth, had attracted her back to the house where her own baby had been born. She was mesmerised. Not only by the sight of him, but also by the love that the new parents had for each other and their baby. She loved to gaze on a scene, denied her in her own life, but was especially drawn to watching Nathan in his cot at night. It was extremely moving to be part of her emotionally charged energy, but I had to be firm with her, saying that she could not stay as it was unsettling both the baby and the new parents. She was reluctant to heed my words and we remained silent in each other's company. Then she spoke again, saying that she would leave if I promised to pass on a message to the young father. Hesitantly I agreed. She asked me to tell Lee to always be there for his new family, unlike her lover who hadn't been able to do this. Promising to pass this message on, a peaceful energy filled the room as she left.

Keeping a promise

Needless to say, I didn't delay in meeting him, calling to the house two days later. Luckily Anne was visiting her parents with Nathan for a few hours and I explained what had happened and relayed the message from the young woman. Lee accepted the whole incident really well and agreed to keep the promise.

Thankfully this was the end of this young family's encounter with the spirit world and they are still very happy to this day. I visit them regularly and have watched Nathan grow into a beautiful young boy surrounded by love and laughter and I can't help but wonder how different this experience is to the story lived through so many years ago.

5

Past Life Regression

Past lives

There are many people who believe we have all lived numerous lives and that through meditation it is possible to access them. Fascinating as this subject may sound, this was never something I ever had any great desire to explore. This could possibly be because it is also said that when people delve into their past lives, they can often witness their various deaths. If this wasn't enough to put me off, there is another common belief that fears we carry in this life, such as being afraid of the dark, a dislike for tight necklines or becoming distressed when underwater, are all signs that we were either drowned or strangled in a past life. Since I have a dislike for all three, I have never had an interest in exploring this possibility in case I witnessed some unimaginable horror that would haunt me for the rest of my life. Along with this though, a part of me was unconvinced by the argument of an ability to regress into the past. But then I had to re-examine my views on this topic several years ago after experiencing something very unusual in the beautiful city of Dubrovnik in Croatia.

I was visiting Dubrovnik with Thomas and some friends for a summer holiday. Dubrovnik is a unique town, rebuilt after a devastating assault by air, land and sea in the Baltic war of 1992. The town suffered terrible casualties and extensive structural damage, but we had heard of its great beauty and the attempts made to rebuild it to its former glory and decided to visit.

One afternoon, Thomas and I were inside the old walled town alone and we decided to visit the war museum. It was a beautiful summer's day and as we made our way through the streets, we noticed a large group of people gathered in the central square, with some rather haunting music rising from within their midst. Curious as always, we ventured closer, weaving our way through the crowd until we came across three men dressed in traditional Indian clothes playing pan pipes. The music was quite beautiful and we were soon entranced as the sounds drifted above us, echoing off the surrounding buildings and churches. The men finished their tune while we all clapped and cheered, hopefully waiting for another. They obliged us by turning their attention to some sets of Indian drums. Two of them began banging on them loudly and the tempo of the music changed. The third man then began to perform some kind of Indian dance, moving slowly around in circles, singing a traditional song in time with the drum beat. My relaxed enjoyment of the music ended abruptly at this point, as I became alive with waves of tingling energy that swept through my whole body with the strongest force I had ever known up to that point. It was so powerful that I thought I would surely fall over, feeling as though I was struggling to stand upright. I was even concentrating on my breathing, trying to keep it calm and even. The dancing had taken my breath away. While struggling with all of these strange sensations I was acutely aware that not only did I recognise the music, but more importantly, his dance, even though I had never seen or heard either before. Watching, mesmerised, I followed his movements, recognising each dip in his body, swing of his arm or shuffle of his feet. Hypnotised by the distinctive sound of the song he was chanting, the people and even Thomas faded into the background, my mind now locked somewhere in the past in a place I recognised yet did not know. Somewhere I felt a deep connection to and a sense of belonging. I longed for him to continue chanting and dancing forever. But why? Could it be true, that we have all been on this earth before in other lifetimes? Was it possible for the memories of these lives to remain locked within us, activated by the right trigger?

I did not have to wait long to discover the answers to all these questions, when one day I unexpectedly took part in a past life regression.

I was attending a one-day group workshop in a nearby city. I had no idea past life work was part of the programme. As far as I was aware it was a meditation workshop. I am not sure that the facilitator planned it either, it just happened when people were chatting about spirits and she asked if we would like to try a past life regression. Everyone else agreed eagerly, but I didn't know what to do. Other than getting up and walking out of the room, I was obviously going to have to take part. Before I could gather my thoughts, the facilitator had begun a meditation that would lead us into the past. Knowing my chance to leave had passed, I spent most of the initial meditation frantically calling in as many angels as I could possibly muster at any one time to protect me, even adding the spirits of my grandfather and Uncle Denis for good measure.

Past life regression

In order to leave the world as we know it and go back in time, we were told to imagine stepping backwards, allowing ourselves to free fall until we felt as though we landed on the ground. Nervously taking the step back, I felt myself falling for what felt a very long time. In fact I was still falling when the facilitator began speaking again, continuing the meditation with the rest of the group, presuming we were all ready to continue. Eventually, landing with a bump, I knew that I had travelled back in time a very long way. Glancing around me, I found that I was a young girl of about seven or eight years, very similar to how I had been when I did the first healing with Gretta and I had stood beside the angel. This time I was barefoot.

While we might presume that this meant the little girl was poor, the opposite was in fact true. I got a clear sense that she was from a very well to do family and much loved. Attempting to adjust my energy to where I now was, I became aware of a deep, heavy, rumbling beneath the earth and while of course it is impossible for history to repeat itself, somehow I knew that a scene from the past was about to be replayed so I could understand the full story.

Prior to my arrival the child had been playing happily outside in the countryside, some distance away from her family home. It was a much warmer climate than I am used to and being barefoot was usual. As she played alone in the fields picking flowers, there was a devastating earthquake. I did not see the moment of the quake. I was only given the sensation of rumbling underfoot. Instinct told the child not to return home but to run, as swiftly as possible into the nearby mountains and to climb as high and as fast as she could. In terror, she fled deep into a nearby wood on a mountainside as mayhem followed her, climbing higher and higher to escape harm. I was so worried for her safety and as I watched her running I thought I was going to see a terrible tragedy. But I did not. I knew the earthquake destroyed everything the child held dear. Not just her family and friends, but all familiar landmarks, her home and even her town. Perhaps my trepidation for her safety interfered somewhat with the energy of the story, as the regression seemed to take a change, leaving the little girl and entering another person's lifetime. There was a slight confusion of energy when this happened, almost like when trying to find a radio station. Now I could clearly see an old woman. She also seemed to be in a forest, quite similar to the one the girl had run into, except this hill seemed much steeper. The old lady had spent nearly her whole life living alone amongst the trees, yet I knew she was content. The animals of the forest were her friends and she lived very simply in a shack where she survived until well into her eighties. The change in the story threw me somewhat, as I did not know what happened to the child, but I certainly didn't get the gruesome ending that I had been dreading.

When the meditation came to an end we were invited to share our experiences. I told everyone of my initial reluctance to take part in the exercise, but of how this amazing visualisation had unfolded before me and everyone agreed that it was an extraordinary experience.

Not long after this I was sitting down to lunch with my two sons, something that was becoming a rarity as they had now both left home, when I decided to tell them about the past life regression exercise. They were intrigued, and since the facilitator had given me a copy of the meditation, I asked if they would like to try it, knowing they were far more adventurous than me. Both said yes, and I decided to join in too. After putting on the CD we settled around the kitchen table and then slowly drifted into the same guided meditation that I had followed previously.

I was much more relaxed this time, knowing exactly

what to expect. Taking a step backwards, I began to free fall. This time the fall was much shorter and on looking round, I found myself standing in the middle of a meadow. Glancing around, everything was bathed in glorious sunshine and once again I had become part of a world that was much warmer than where I now live. Familiarising myself with the landscape, I was stunned by its natural beauty, untouched by either man or machine. Standing in the middle of the meadow was a beautiful young woman of about nineteen years of age. I became aware that she was heartbroken, staring into the distance before her. I followed her gaze which led to a large forest. Not sure what was wrong, once again I was given an opportunity to witness previous events. The young woman had been arguing with her lover. I'm not sure what the quarrel was about or why they were standing in the middle of a meadow when they had it, but I have a feeling it was a place they often met. Whatever took place on this particular day caused the young man to mount his horse in a blinding rage, and ride off into the forest. Of course, as in the case of many a lovers' tiff, harsh words are spoken in anger which were soon regretted. At these times all that matters is to receive the unspoken words of forgiveness found in a warm embrace and this quarrel was no different. Unfortunately there was no chance of forgiveness as the young man never came back.

Day after day she returned to the meadow hoping he would be there, until she did so just to cling to the memory of the last time she had seen him. Watching the scene was so sad. Her heartache was palpable. She could not believe that he did not return and neither could I. Where was he? She thought he had adored her, as she did him. Because of her beauty, she had many other admirers, but her heart was taken and as the years passed, I knew she never loved again.

As we came out of the meditation I was devastated for the young woman. Her sorrow and mourning had hung around her like a heavy wet coat. I don't even remember what the boys told me about their experience of the meditation, as I was so caught up within my own story and I longed to be able to help her.

Later that night while turning over in bed, I saw the young man from the story standing silently beside me. While trying to rouse my sleepy mind to form a coherent sentence of greeting, he spoke first and I heard his side of the story from the moment when he mounted the horse and rode off into the forest. He told me that as he galloped through the trees in a blinding rage, he had been less cautious than usual. After a couple of miles of riding, he had hit his head on a low bough of a tree, fell from his horse and died instantly.

The young girl never heard of his death as he was from another town quite a distance from her own and his family knew nothing of their meetings. He told me that if the accident had not happened he would have returned to her as she thought he would, for he had loved her beyond words. He was aware of her distress and had come to me in the hope that she could now rest in peace, knowing that he had loved her deeply and that he forgave her for slighting him that day. I promised him that this message would be passed on, although somehow I was aware that the story was already being relayed to her through me.

Whatever my previous thoughts had been about past life regression, it certainly hadn't been this. Could I still deny it as a possibility? How had these stories opened up to me through a simple meditation? Were there millions of other stories floating around on some invisible plane, or had I simply opened myself up to the spirit world once more, so that stories from the past could filter through. One thing was certain. I could relate to all three of these stories. As a child, I loved to roam in the country lanes, picking wild flowers. I could readily relate to the old woman's love of animals. As for a broken heart? Well, that too had been part of my life and I hate saying goodbye to loved ones. Could the similarities of the three stories that related to my own personality just be an amazing coincidence, or is it possible that we hold memories from past lifetimes within us, all pieced together like an invisible jigsaw, making us the person we are today.

6

Angels

$\mathcal{A}$lthough I.E.T.® is associated with the whole experience of angels, I never really expected to see one, let alone many. I feel that celestial beings appear to people in a way that they can easily interpret. As I come from a Christian upbringing, it seemed natural that it was through the identification of angels that I was able to communicate with a higher entity. For those of different faiths, celestial beings probably appear in other forms, so that they too can be easily recognisable.

Channelling energy from angels is a fascinating experience and their messages are surprisingly precise. They phrase their words very differently from my way of speaking and are therefore distinct from my own thoughts. This makes them very easy to pass on to whomever they are intended. Once the message is relayed, the thought immediately leaves my consciousness and, no matter how hard I try, I cannot recall it. Because of this, I either use my dictaphone to record anything I hear, or before channelling, those around me are advised to take note of anything I may say, as I won't be able to repeat it afterwards. I actually quite like this process, as many of the messages are very private and, if the truth be told, none of my business. Being a private sort of person myself, I find this very respectful of the angels as well as to those who are receiving the messages. It leaves me to act only as a vessel, which I am more than happy to do.

Angels have wonderfully vivid colours swirling around them and without exception, are lovely to gaze upon. This is how I have come to understand that angelic energy, which ever way one may interpret it, can only be for the good. Quite simply, from every encounter I have had with them, it is clear that angels are a representation of pure love. There appears to be no conformity to their appearance, yet I am always aware of their eyes, sometimes their faces, hands, bodies, clothing and wings, yet never their feet.

I have never been able to 'touch' an angel – although I have tried, by putting my hand out when one is standing before me. Their wings can vary enormously and an angel's height does not necessarily determine the size, volume, or even weight of their wings. Their wings can be multicoloured, white, or have a translucent iridescence. Sometimes they are beautiful and softly feathered; other times they resemble wings of butterflies or moths, but on a much larger scale. Their wings can be open or closed and are sometimes moving swiftly or very gently.

Interestingly, I have never seen angels use wings or feet in their approach. Somehow they just come into focus, visible to me through the third eye. I have pondered on this fact repeatedly, finally concluding that this is simply because they do not actually come from anywhere – their energy is all around us; we share and live within the same time and space. Until developing my psychic ability, like many others, I simply couldn't feel or recognise their energy.

If this were true, then what are their wings for? Perhaps I interpret angels in this way simply because this is how I learned to recognise an angel as a child, assuming that to live in the heavens, one would of course need wings to fly.

The way in which angels appear to move is remarkable in its simplicity. Angels' movement is an expansion of their core energy. Once I am able to see them clearly, they can appear to move closer. To do this, an angel doesn't actually move at all, but simply expands its energy to encompass distance, therefore appearing closer.

They can vary in shape and form, from a human adult's size to that of gigantic beings that seem to fill the sky. Many angels appear to leave gifts before they go and often flowers are placed upon my knees or in my hair. One of the most beautiful angels had long flowing hair that was formed from the purple flowers of a climbing purple wisteria and her dress had a train of peacock feathers trailing behind her. She was simply stunning to see.

Angels' eyes are impossibly beautiful. Whatever their shade or shape, they seem to hold my attention within some kind of unspoken communication. One day, in finding it nearly impossible to convey their beauty to others I decided to ask them directly for help. Their response was to emphasize and focus on the unconditional love that comes through their eyes and all their messages. Taken aback by the speed and clarity of their reply, I thanked them for their help and quickly scribbled down the message on a piece of paper so I wouldn't forget it.

Other messages I have received were also clearly stated. *As we listen, watch and wait, our love never falters.* Another message channelled to me was: *Angels' eyes are all-seeing, all-knowing, yet never judging.* I was right. Their help had been needed, I could never have found words such as these to describe them. They were simplicity itself, yet profound in meaning.

I have come to understand that all the different vibrations that I recognise – be they spirits, cherubs, fairies, animal spirits, tree energy, or angels – coexist around us within their own realms. They are available and accessible to everyone, yet for some reason most of us can't perceive these realities.

It could be compared to how we use our gift of sight to observe the world around us. When we wish to observe something outside of our physical range, such as stars in the night sky, we use binoculars or a telescope. Without these, we are inclined to turn away, unable to distinguish specific detail.

I believe the energy of celestial beings follows a similar concept. It can be understood to exist beyond our own energy fields or auras and therefore our five senses cannot attune to this frequency, making many believe it simply does not exist. For those who can sense the presence of angelic energy, there seems to be quite a bit of variation in how it is experienced. I 'see' these energetic vibrations through my third eye, while Lee 'feels' their energy and Thomas 'sees' them with his physical eye. Thomas says that if he lets his eyes relax without focusing on anything in particular, he is able to see specks of light everywhere, similar to television static. He explained further that all these specks have different intensities, densities and colours, depending on where they are or who they are around. Out of these specks of light, various beings gradually come into focus for him, resembling people and animals.

Most people seem to have at least a subtle awareness that different forms of energy exist beyond what can be seen or felt with the five senses. Countless books have been written about these worlds and many millions have read them, longing to see, be part of, or find some proof that these worlds exist. Until my experiences began I had no interest in having these concepts explained to me. I merely thought of them as part of a fantasy world, such as the one my mother portrayed to me through bedtime stories as I drifted off to sleep as a child.

As an adult, I have read just one book about angels and only after my own experiences began to occur. My story of connecting to the angelic realm emerged without any outside influences and was simply initiated by the attunement and heartlinking process we learned on the I.E.T.® course.

I am aware that many angels are known by specific names and that many people get great comfort from the fact that they can call on a particular angel for any given situation. I was once shown a bewildering list of such names to call on in an array of situations, but find this far too confusing. I have never worked with the angels in this way, except in the case of Archangel Michael, whom I call on for strength and protection whenever I am feeling particularly nervous.

Rather than seeking out specific angels, my best advice is to allow the right angel for any given situation to come to you. They know exactly who is needed at any given time.

People also often ask me to describe angels more clearly to them, but, without the ability to paint or draw, this has always been frustratingly difficult. Then one day my dilemma was, in some way resolved in the strangest of places. I was on the London Underground with Thomas waiting for a tube to arrive. From the busy platform, I idly glanced at the large billboards on the opposite side of the line. Staring right back at me from one of these posters was an image of a woman who was almost an exact interpretation of how I see many of the angels. I could scarcely believe my eyes, nor contain my excitement.

Normally when I communicate with angels, I have little time to observe their beauty in any great detail, as I am listening carefully to what they are saying. Here though, in the hustle and bustle of rush hour, I could gaze at this image for as long as I liked, if I didn't mind missing the next tube.

Thomas had left briefly to dispose of some rubbish. When he returned, I excitedly told him my news, the words falling over each other in my excitement. I asked him if he recognised the image, not expecting for one minute that he would. To my surprise, he told me that he did and that it was Pre-Raphaelite art. He explained that there were many similar paintings from this era which he could show me later online. He also told me in no uncertain terms that he had no intention of staying on the platform one minute longer than necessary so that I could gaze at a poster, as it was unbearably hot and noisy. Therefore a few moments later, I stood inside a stuffy, tightly packed tube beside him, but I was hardly aware of the crowd or the intense heat. At long last I had found an image that revealed how I see the beauty of the angels.

Although many angels I see have a Pre-Raphaelite appearance, other times I see them as similar to how they are depicted on the stained-glass windows or statues in churches around the world. After I started seeing angels, I began to look at such works of art more closely. Gazing at biblical scenes, including angels and cherubs, I realised that I was witnessing the same visualisation that artists have been interpreting over many centuries. Did this mean that for thousands of years others were able to see and hear as I do? Were the painters and sculptors as stunned as I by this extraordinary ability to observe and communicate with an energy that was not visible to the physical eye? Did they tell others? Were they ridiculed or persecuted for their beliefs, or did they stay quiet as I longed to.

As such thoughts filled my mind, I was reminded of Joan of Arc whose name I took for my confirmation at ten years of age. My mother was very surprised at the time, as she thought it an unlikely choice of saint for one so young. Yet I remember only being incredibly impressed by Joan of Arc's bravery when I read about her in religion class at school.

Joan of Arc was an illiterate peasant girl who lived in the small village of Domrémy in France with her parents on their fifty-acre farm. She was born in 1412, at a time when France was gripped by the Hundred Year War, which began in 1337 between the French and British over the French throne. By 1429, the war had devastated the French economy, which had not yet recovered from the Black Death of the previous century. This combination had isolated France from foreign markets and investments and the English had by this point nearly achieved their objective of a dual monarchy. Most of northern and southwest France was under British rule, but Joan's village belonged to a small area of Eastern France that remained loyal to the French crown.

At the age of twelve, Joan began to see angelic figures while out in the fields, later identifying them as Saint Michael, Saint Catherine and Saint Margaret. She described them as being so beautiful that when they left her, she cried. These saints told her that she was to save France from the continuing English invasion and to bring Charles VII to the throne. Incredibly, at the age of 15 and dressed as a page boy so as not to bring unnecessary attention to herself, she gained entry to the royal French court. She achieved this through persistence, insisting she be allowed to talk to a member of authority, and by an accurate prediction she gave about a military reversal near Orleans.

One can only guess at the morale of the French court at this time, considering that because of this prediction, they allowed someone so young to lead their armies into battle, based on messages she alleged were from God. Although she was an uneducated peasant, she is recorded as having a remarkable intellect, far beyond her years and it is believed by many that it was this intelligence rather than her battle skills that led the French to several important victories against the English.

At eighteen years of age Joan was captured by the Burgundians, a pro-English group, who sold her to the English. Without any attempt by the French to intervene on her behalf, the English tried Joan as a heretic. Faced with torture and death, she refused at her trial to answer questions about her messages from the saints and God. At the age of nineteen, she was convicted and burnt at the stake and her ashes were then thrown into the River Seine.

Even now I find her story almost too incredible to believe and take in. How had she found such unimaginable courage to face battle alongside an army of hardened soldiers at such a young age, based on messages given to her from saints? Where did she find the faith and trust in her young heart to follow these messages through? If it wasn't so well-documented in history, it would seem unbelievable. While on the subject of belief, now that angels were speaking directly to me, where was my courage, faith, and trust in them to follow through on whatever I was supposed to do, even though I was still totally unaware of what it was? I hadn't told people within my community, never mind a whole country. The gruesome fate of many apostles and saints, including Joan, was hardly an incentive to share the news of my gift with others. Interestingly, Joan is the patron saint of those who are persecuted for their spiritual beliefs and an inspiration to anyone who feels a call to help yet worries about being able to make a difference.

Had I subconsciously known at ten years of age that one day I would need her strength of character as an example to draw on? This was beginning to feel like more of a distinct possibility as time went by, as courage and strength were qualities I seriously lacked in regard to accepting my own abilities. It wasn't as if I was now part of something that everyone could relate to or understand. Why hadn't I been as clearly guided as Joan of Arc? When she received messages from saints, she had also been able to see them clearly standing before her. Would I have been more inclined to listen to them if I could also have seen them with my physical eye rather than my third eye? All these questions raged endlessly in my head as I desperately sought answers.

Archangel Michael

It seems that Archangel Michael eventually took pity on my inner angst, as a huge turning point in my abilities came about, once again, right out of the blue. I was in Rome at the time with Thomas on a week's holiday. I had always wanted to go there and since he liked the study of architecture, we knew we would enjoy each other's company in this incredibly cultured capital. Halfway through our stay, we decided to take a detour from our planned day's schedule and crossed a bridge called Ponte Sant'Angelo.

As we strolled across in the sunshine, we stopped to look at the souvenirs displayed by the vendors who had set up along the length of the bridge. I bought quite a few gifts here, as many of the products were handmade and unique. One particular vendor, noticing our genuine interest in his goods told us of a small outdoor market that also sold handmade products. He pointed across the river in the direction where we should go and as we squinted against the sun, trying to see which way he was pointing, something caught my eye.

On top of a large, dome-shaped building at the end of the bridge was a huge statue of Archangel Michael, whom I recognised instantly as how he appears to me. I thought the sun must have been playing tricks and shielded my eyes to get a better look. I was so used to only seeing him through my third eye, that to see him physically seemed impossible to believe. For one ridiculous moment I almost shouted out: 'What on earth are you doing up there?'

Yet gazing down across the streets of Rome, was someone who appeared beside me whenever I needed reassurance in the strange reality I was now living in. Almost in a trance I continued along the bridge, unable to take my eyes off the statue. Thomas, noticing my interest shift from the market to the building before us, asked if I wanted to go in. *Did I want to go in? I wanted to go up to the top of the building to the statue as soon as was humanly possible.*

We soon learned from the history guides at the admission gate that we were standing in the Castel Sant'Angelo or Castle of the Holy Angel. This impressive building is the mausoleum of Hadrian, who had it built to hold his ashes after his death, between 135 and 139 AD. He also had the Ponte Sant'Angelo bridge built to connect the mausoleum to the city. Legend has it that in the year 590, Archangel Michael appeared on the top of the building, sheathing his sword as a sign of the end of the plague. In 1536, a statue of Archangel Michael was erected on top of the building, which was then replaced in 1753 by the present one.

This statue held special significance for me simply because it was a confirmation that what was happening to me was not only real, but had happened to others, too. Whereas discovering Pre-Raphaelite art enabled me to describe the appearance of the angels I see, the statue in some way felt more personal. It was as if Archangel Michael was saying,

'Here, look at me, I am real, I do come to see you,' but, more importantly, 'others have seen me, too.' Up to this point, I had been reluctant to share the experience of Archangel Michael with anyone. I felt sure people would think I had gone quite mad if I told them there was an angel who carried a sword.

Yet here I was, gazing up at Archangel Michael standing majestically over the city of Rome, as he had appeared to people many centuries ago in this exact spot. For the first time I allowed myself the luxury of believing that I really was able to communicate with angelic beings.

Had Archangel Michael deliberately led us across the bridge so I would see him with my naked eye and believe in him? I almost wept at the thought of such a powerful celestial being helping me to accept my gift. Of course being in a strange city surrounded by complete strangers, I did no such thing.

The Sistine Chapel

Another day on that same holiday, we decided to go to St Peter's Square and the Vatican. Luckily, we had been advised to go early to avoid the long queues into the Vatican. First we paid a visit to St Peter's Basilica, which was simply spectacular and then we joined the still-small queue to enter the Vatican. Once inside though, we were surprised to discover that the place was already full of people. We walked along with the crowd, moving almost as one, through the narrow passages admiring the many magnificent paintings and sculptures.

There was so much to look at that there was no way of taking it all in. As we entered the Sistine Chapel, I began to feel frustrated by the sheer number of people around me. It was impossible to move at one's own pace. Fortunately, we managed to disentangle ourselves from the body of people when we spotted a space on a bench that lined the chapel's walls. I don't think I have ever been so glad to sit down in my whole life. At last, I could actually take stock of where I was and what I was seeing.

The incomparable artwork of Michelangelo surrounded us on all the walls and ceilings. It was hard to find words to describe his talent and I was mesmerized by the shade of green he had used. It was exquisite and reminded me of new leaves on trees as they burst from their buds. In fact the scenes he depicted were so real that one could almost imagine being a part of the heavens above.

I say almost, as there were still large parties of people moving through the room, talking constantly, despite regular pleas over the intercom for silence in the chapel. I sighed loudly in exasperation. If only it were possible to come back early of a morning to enjoy the room alone. With this thought, the energy of the room began to change. I wasn't sure how at first, yet I knew something was happening. The crowd was still talking loudly and the voice was still asking for silence. No-one else seemed to be aware of the change. Turning to Thomas I asked in a whisper if he had noticed it. He nodded his head and put his finger to his lips. I then sat quietly beside him, waiting for whatever was about to happen, glad he was beside me.

The sounds in the crowded chapel started to fade somehow and other people's presence seemed to be, in some way, pushed back until they became almost invisible. Trying to understand this phenomenon, I became aware of the presence of an enormous pure white being of light, straight across the room from us. As I watched, the expansion of its energy increased so that it appeared to grow larger and closer – until it was right before us.

I am not sure if it was an angel, although I presumed it must be, considering where we were, but instinctively knew that it was powerful within its own realm. I was stunned that one so influential would want to make contact with us. There was no exchange of words, it was almost like a meeting of souls and we communicated at a level that was beyond my comprehension. I still cannot find the words to describe what passed between us, but it felt like an acknowledgement from a celestial world to ours and all I could think of at the time was – what a perfect place to do it.

Back to the shop

I hadn't forgotten my promise to return to Sally if, or when, I found Gretta McCarthy. After our visit to Rome, I dutifully returned for my third and final visit, ringing beforehand to ensure that my return coincided with one of her visits. She remembered me straight away. Recounting how I had found Gretta McCarthy and taken part in the I.E.T.® course, I asked if she would like a heartlink and she immediately agreed. Much energy passed between us once I had established my connection to the angels and she was moved to comment on how peaceful it felt. Turning to the shop assistant Sue, who was also in the room, out of politeness more than anything else, I asked if she would also like to have one. This offer was accepted, while Sally asked if she could sit and watch. I was more than happy to oblige, extremely curious to know what she would see.

After the heartlink I turned excitedly to Sally for her interpretation, but she looked totally taken aback. She explained that after the heartlink began, a beam of light had poured out of the top of my head and that then another much stronger beam of white light had returned through the back of my head at a slight angle. She then continued, saying that from my chest, another beam of light was formed to Sue sitting opposite me. Yet, what was most amazing of all was the sight of huge white wings on my back. There was dead silence in the shop at this revelation and I'm sure we could have heard a pin drop as we all sat staring speechlessly at each other. What could this mean?

I never got the chance to return to the shop after this visit, as shortly after it closed down. I've always found it curious that, before being given the voucher at Christmas, I had not known of its existence and now that I had returned to the shop as promised, it then closed down – and I never heard of Sally the medium again.

Wings

The whole concept of having a pair of wings seemed to

be just too far-fetched for me, so I didn't trouble my sons with this latest revelation. It's not that I didn't believe Sally, as why else would she have said it; it just seemed beyond belief. I decided that maybe it was about time I did something normal, with perfectly normal people for a change. But this hope was shattered one evening as I sat watching TV with Thomas.

We were happily relaxed in each other's company after a long day, when he casually asked me to put my wings away.

'What!' I shouted, nearly falling off the settee. 'What do you mean – put my wings away I haven't got any!' my voice rose hysterically with each word. Quite calmly and without taking his eyes off the television, he told me that obviously I now had, since they were annoying him as he could see them from the corner of his eye. Trying to remain as calm as he was clearly able to, nervously I asked,

'How on earth do you put wings away?'

This question managed to distract him enough to look away from the television to state that he had absolutely no idea, since he had never noticed them before. After a moment's pause he did suggest trying to visualise folding them up and then went back to watching the film. With my quiet night in tatters, I did as he suggested and then tentatively asked him if they had gone. Thankfully they had.

7

Life Before the Gift Token

Until I reached my mid-twenties, it would be safe to say that nothing particularly out of the ordinary happened in my life. I was born in the County of Lancashire in England, the youngest of four children. I grew up alongside my sister and two brothers in Bury, a bustling market town overlooked by the magnificent Lancashire moors, which separate Lancashire from Yorkshire.

For many hundreds of years this area was part of a large royal hunting forest called the Forest of Blackburnshire, but in 1507 King Henry VII decreed that the area should be deforested for settlements and cultivation. As the land became habitable, people began to settle into the area, but farming proved to be quite difficult as much of the land was moorland, making a sustainable living hard to maintain. With the advent of the Industrial Revolution a large cotton and woollen industry grew and thrived in the region. The area had access to the

Liverpool Docks via the River Irwell and the Manchester Ship Canal, allowing for direct trade with America. Our town, situated beside the River Irwell, was very much part of that era, and many of the local people would have been employed by the rich mill owners. As many people came to settle and work in the area, the need to feed large families grew and a huge outdoor market arose. Every week since 1853 the town has burst into life as traders from all over the county bring products to sell from over 200 stalls.

From an early age the hustle and bustle of a typical market day was part of my life. Clutching Mother's hand, I trailed behind her as she haggled with the traders, jostling through hundreds of other people among the small alleyways that separated each row of stalls.

Another early memory is of the moors themselves. Our parents often took us up to Ashworth Moors to 'stretch our legs'. These moors are wild, windy, isolated and quite barren, but I grew to love them as we explored every rock, crevice and stream that ran down to the rivers below. We visited in every season, knowing them in the biting autumn winds, the deep snow of winter, the coolness of spring and the beautiful warmth of summer. The moment we arrived at 'Owd Betts', we would scramble from the car, savouring the rush of the wind pulling at our hair and clothes. We scampered along the rough pathways and through the bracken, lost in our own world. I remember a sense of freedom and belonging within them that seemed to fill my being. Here I felt truly happy.

Alicia

At three years of age I met Alicia when I cycled past her house on my small tricycle. Alicia, who was also three, lived four doors down from our house, and from that first encounter, a strong friendship developed. We were inseparable and this friendship carried us through the next twenty-two years until I left England to live in Ireland and she went to London to pursue her career. But this was all still to come and at the tender age of three, all that mattered was having fun; so with my siblings in school, we became inseparable playmates.

When I was four years of age, this idyllic existence was somewhat disrupted when I was sent off to the local Catholic primary school, along with a weary-looking leather satchel containing an even wearier-looking apple from the garden. Alicia, on the other hand, was sent to the Church of England school 'up the hill'. I remember demanding to know why I couldn't go to school with her. The answer from my parents was vague and I was soon trudging back and forth to school alongside my siblings, while Alicia walked to school in the opposite direction. Thankfully, I settled into this new routine and my days at school made for many happy memories. I also made new friends. Nevertheless, an invisible line was drawn between school friends and Alicia that I never allowed anyone to cross. The minute I returned home from school, we were back outside together again, playing as we always had.

These primary school years passed in a blur of teachers' names and faces, blackboards, white chalk, dusters and skipping in the street. As well as learning the core curriculum, I learnt to dance, scrape torturously at my Uncle Tom's violin for six years, and attempted to sing in the church choir.

When we finished primary school, Alicia and I were thankfully reunited at the town's grammar school. To make sure this happened, we solemnly promised that we would pass our eleven plus examination, which would enable us to be together. With this accomplished and my life now complete again, secondary school carried on in a similar pattern to my primary education, except now I walked to school with Alicia, played sports for the school, sang in the yearly school musical, and Uncle Tom's violin took a well-earned rest.

Influenced by the values of my parents and teachers, I learnt the norms of society and understood which behaviours were acceptable and which were not. I grew up to respect invisible yet distinct boundaries, which influenced my way of thinking and behaviour. I knew right from wrong, good from bad. In other words, I developed a reasonably healthy social consciousness. This served me well, and I progressed into a stereotypical individual from Western society. I finished school, sat my exams, went on to college and began to work.

Religion also featured strongly in our home and again I followed an unspoken format. We went to mass every

Sunday and on church holidays. I made my first Confession, Holy Communion and Confirmation. I got married in the same church I had attended all my life, and my two children were baptised in the same font as I had been. I then in turn, took them to church and the same cycle began again. I had passed every test of socially acceptable and moral behaviour with flying colours.

Everything seemed to be in order, or was it? On the surface my life appeared to be perfect according to how it should be, but in my heart I felt a restlessness I did not understand. Although I could not fully comprehend the feeling, I was aware that it was something far beyond any of the lessons I had been taught so far. Somehow, something had not yet been explained to me.

This felt very frustrating as everything in my life seemed to be in order. I had no idea how to unlock this unexplained level of consciousness as I had no understanding of it. Looking back over my life, I did in fact acknowledge this 'calling', but it is only now that I am aware that I was doing so.

Forgotten flowers

From an early age without being aware of it, I was attached to nature and some of my earliest memories are connected to the fate of flowers and animals. One such memory includes a big cherry blossom tree that stood in a far corner of our back garden. Each May this tree celebrated life by producing an abundance of pink blossoms that hung in heavy bunches. It was a particularly beautiful sight, but also a very busy and somewhat stressful time for one particular young lady. I loved this tree with a passion and was always terribly upset when the blossoms began to fall from the branches long before they had died, usually due to wind or rain.

Because of this I spent most of the month of May running in and out the house rescuing the delicate bunches. Every available glass, pot, jug, egg cup and saucer was put to use as I ferried the flowers inside so that they wouldn't die, unnoticed, on the ground outside. This process took place in all kinds of inclement weather. When I think back, my mother's patience must have been tested to the limit with these annual proceedings, yet she never uttered a word, only producing more containers for the fading flowers.

Another early memory is of being a bridesmaid at my cousin's wedding when I carried a posy of flowers that were in a round ball hanging down from a long ribbon. I distinctly remember that they were pink and also how very unhappy I was when we returned home after the wedding still clutching my posy. This unhappiness was due to the fact that I knew the flowers were going to die. I was only four years old at the time, yet I remember this dismay clearly. Once more my mother came to the rescue and suggested that we plant the posy in the garden to see if it might grow. Together we went out into the garden and planted the posy in the soil, quite near the cherry blossom tree, and I was placated ... for the time being.

This strong bond with nature extended far beyond flowers, since I also had the same sympathetic view towards animals and insects. During the long school summer holidays, as we whiled away endless idle days, wandering down country lanes under a hot sun, I would spend hours saving flies that were drowning in puddles. This sounds ridiculous now, but at the time it was anything but.

When I think back now, I must have had the patience of a saint as I searched for long twigs that I pushed into deep puddles formed by the heavy weight of tractor wheels, to catch as many drowning flies as I could. I would then leave the twig somewhere safe for the flies to dry off and fly away. Sometimes, if time allowed, I would sit observing the miraculous drying process, as each soddened leg and wing being dried by the heat of the sun, brought these tiny beings of creation back to life. I never seemed to tire of watching this transformation take place before my young eyes.

It was no summer pastime that drove these rescue operations, but a strong overriding instinct to help an animal in need. I was teased mercilessly by my siblings for this daily ritual and was told to catch up and continue with whatever I was supposed to be doing; usually blackberry-picking for mother to make jam. But I didn't care what anyone thought, or how much I was teased; to me there was nothing more important to be doing than saving helpless animals' lives.

Apache

When I was about ten years old I decided it was time we had a family pet. Neither of my parents were pet lovers, so this proved to be a particularly difficult objective to achieve. I tried the usual child-like begging, pleading with them endlessly for a cat or dog, but to no avail. My brothers decided to join me in my endless lament, but we couldn't budge our parents an inch. I had to think. I was going to have to approach this problem from a different angle, but I had no idea how.

The solution came totally out of the blue and involved the death of my grandfather. It was a lovely Saturday morning in summer and I went outside to enjoy the sunshine. As I wandered around the garden I heard a very faint sound that I was barely able to recognise. Stopping, I listened closely and heard it again. This time I knew exactly what it was, the tiny meow of a small kitten. I stood still, hardly daring to breathe as I waited to hear the sound once more so I could gauge where it was coming from. I was soon scouring the hedges like a detective following the plaintive call until I came across a kitten of about eight weeks old staring up at me. I fell to my knees before it in delight and it came straight over to me to be petted. It was a beautiful kitten with white, black and ginger markings all over its body. I sat to play with it for about fifteen minutes before scooping it up and heading back to the house full of intent.

I needed to think, and think fast, before I reached the

back door … and my mother. I played out the forthcoming scenario in my mind. Would her heart melt when she saw the beautiful kitten in my arms? I tried to imagine my mother's face melting, and decided this was very unlikely. In panic, I tried out another scenario. Would I hide it in the garden shed and feed it there, hoping that no one would find it? This had endless problems attached to it. Getting desperate I tried again: would I offer to do all the household chores for the rest of my life and beyond if I could keep it? All kinds of possibilities were racing through my mind as I reached the house. Feeling slightly nervous I put the kitten down on the ground and whispered for it to behave, then opened the back door and went in.

Mother as always was in the kitchen, and when I saw her I tried desperately to remember which story I had decided to tell her. Nervously clearing my throat, I decided to tell her the truth. I was half way through my tale, watching her rolling out some pastry, when the telephone rang. Wiping her hands on a nearby cloth, she left the room to answer it and I threw myself onto a kitchen chair in dismay. Any success of even getting to finish my tale very much depended on who was on the other end of the phone, how long the call might take and what mood my mother might be in after it. Gloomily chewing on a piece of raw pastry, I waited for her return. She came back much quicker than I had expected and I was surprised to see that she was crying. I quickly went over to ask what was wrong and she told me that her brother had just rung to say her father had died that morning.

I put my arms around her as she cried, at a loss as to what to do or say next. Everyone else was out, so I couldn't holler down the hallway for some much needed support. Since I was obviously going to have to deal with this crisis on my own, I did what everyone does at times like these and put the kettle on for a cup of tea. Ten minutes later we sat together in silence at the kitchen table cradling our cups for comfort, when from outside we heard the sound of a hesitant meow through an open window. I had completely forgotten all about the kitten. Horrified, I held my breath, not daring to look up at Mother. What dreadful timing for the arrival of a stray kitten.

Unexpectedly and possibly due to her grief, Mother said that as long as the kitten didn't belong to any of our neighbours I could keep it, but only if it never came into the house and slept in the shed. I cannot remember exactly what happened just after that but I am sure I must have struggled to contain my excitement, knowing that this was not the time for any display of happiness.

'Apache', as my mother named the kitten, became part of our family for the next fourteen years. She took an incredibly short time to worm her way into my mother's heart and onto the best chair near the kitchen stove, as only a cat has an inbuilt ability to do. I'm sure I don't need to tell you, as any pet lover would know, that Apache brought laughter and sunshine into our home and fond memories that are cherished forever.

A life between two lives

When I reached my teens, my interest in plants began to extend far beyond the bedroom and developed into a love of gardening. Whereupon until this point my mother would have often gone out gardening alone in the evenings, I was now by her side. I learnt invaluable skills as we tended to the numerous shrubs and flowers and we spent many a happy evening until the sun set, weeding, pruning and picking fruit. Mother had long since spotted my genuine interest in caring for plants and one day asked if I had ever thought of taking up a career linked to horticulture. To be honest I had never given my future any thought at all, but she persisted, and this persistence planted the seeds of an idea that flourished into an ambition to train as a florist when I left school.

Once qualified, I opened a little shop in a small town near home and I worked there for a number of years. It was around this time that the confusing feelings I had always had about there being much more to my life than I had already experienced, began to surface in a way that was impossible to ignore.

A couple of years later I left home to get married and over the next three years gave birth to Lee and Thomas. We also moved to another town, not too far from my home, but further away from the moors. I could no longer see them but knew in which direction they lay, and more often than not I began to find myself staring out of our bedroom window towards them.

As I gazed at the clouds above, I could imagine how their shadows would be drifting slowly across the wide expanse of the barren landscape and I felt a deep longing to be near them again. I felt stifled without them. As though I didn't have enough air to breathe. It felt as if I needed to shake off my human life and be as free as the winds that whipped across the bracken that I knew so well. In my mind's eye, I raced and danced along with the wind as it swirled its wandering fingers around the heather, my feet never touching the ground. I was totally free of all social constraints and conditioning. I felt weightless, my hair was loose and what I wore no longer mattered. It was not as if I was unhappy with my life, far from it. I loved my family dearly and some of my most treasured memories are of this time. I loved walking the three miles back to my parents' home twice a week, pushing a big Silver Cross pram along the roadside with my two little sons tucked safely inside. I have asked if they have any memories of these times, as they are so special to me, but sadly, being so young, neither of them can recollect anything.

Thinking that perhaps I just needed to spend some more time outdoors, I started to take the boys to Heaton Park in Manchester with my father so that we could walk or sit under the magnificent old trees that grace this large, beautiful park. A park where I too had spent many a happy hour in my childhood. But I could not wrestle off this strange longing to be somehow free, in fact it seemed to grow stronger every day.

Eventually I began to tell people that I thought it might be nice to move into the countryside, maybe somewhere near the moors as that was the only way that I could understand what was upsetting me.

In an attempt to appease me, my husband suggested that we go to Ireland to visit some relatives who lived on the coast. Having never been before, I thought that this would be a lovely idea as I had heard how beautiful the Irish countryside was and how it was like taking a step back in time. So in May 1990, we hired a car and under the light of a full moon drove down the motorway to Holyhead and boarded a boat to Dublin. Little did either of us realise the dramatic effect this innocent summer holiday would have on our lives.

It took quite some time to negotiate Dublin when we came off the boat, but since it was late at night this did not present too many difficulties. The two boys were sound asleep in the back of the car and soon we were travelling through the stillness of the night, save for the moonlight shimmering on the unlit roads of the Irish countryside.

Then I became aware of another unusual feeling. The further we travelled, the more obvious it became. It felt as if a heavy weight was being lifted from my whole body, especially from my shoulders, face and out of the top of my head. Sitting silently beside my husband, I tried to fathom out what was happening. Continuing to sit quietly

– in the same way that I am now used to doing when receiving intuitive messages, yet was oblivious to at that time – I began to understand what was taking place.

No one actually spoke to me, I just felt a 'dawning' sensation and everything became crystal clear and I understood perfectly why I had been restless for so long. This was the place where I was supposed to be. It wasn't on the Lancashire moors or sitting under the trees in the park playing with my sons as I had believed. It was here in Ireland, a place I had never even seen before – so how could this be?

Although we had Irish roots and relatives living here, there had never been any reason for me to have a strong bond with Ireland. Yet as I gazed up at the full moon, which continued to monitor our journey, I knew with certainty that this was where I belonged but had no idea why.

Fungi

Our holiday was wonderful. The weather was amazing and for two full weeks we explored all the nooks and crannies of the coastline under a blazing sun. The weather was so beautiful that even now when local people recall that particular May, they remember it as being exceptionally hot.

Nothing out of the ordinary happened throughout our stay until right at the end of the last week when we decided to take a trip around the Ring of Kerry.

Apparently, no trip to Ireland is complete without both this scenic drive and a trip to the town of Dingle in the hope of seeing Fungi, the resident dolphin. It appears that Fungi had been living in Dingle Bay for a number of years. No one knew why he swam into the bay one particular morning, but once he did, he never left again and became a famous tourist attraction.

The Ring of Kerry was simply breathtaking under a clear blue sky, and we thoroughly enjoyed the drive along the coastline of the peninsula, all the way to Dingle, which is quite near the end. Just before we arrived into the town we decided to stroll along the banks of the estuary and stopped to have a picnic, near an old watchtower scrutinising the bay in the hope of a sighting of Fungi. After an hour or so, and with no sign of Fungi, the boys began to get restless. We decided to head into the town where we knew it was possible to take a boat trip out into the bay in the hope of a better chance of seeing him at close quarters. Having parted with our fare, we clambered into a rocking boat, along with about fifteen other people, and, with our skipper on board, set out.

We went out as far as the mouth of the estuary and then before reaching the open sea, turned back towards Dingle. This routine was completed several times, but there was no sign of Fungi. There were no ripples on the water except for the small waves made by our own boat and, if I am honest, I was starting to get fed up. Things weren't helped by the fact that it was a particularly warm day and I was uncomfortably hot and beginning to feel slightly sick from the rocking motion of the boat. As the skipper turned the boat out of the harbour yet again, I reached the point where I could not have cared less whether I saw Fungi or not. Sighing resignedly and in an attempt to distract myself from my increasingly queasy stomach, I leant over the side of the boat and let my hand trail in the water, enjoying the cool sensation rippling against my hand. Suddenly, out of nowhere, Fungi appeared from the depths right beside the boat, and, as his body rose out of the water, the palm of my hand went along the entire length of his back. In that intimate moment between us, as I felt the cold, wet smoothness of his body, I had an unexplainable urge to dive into the water and follow him. For the few moments that my hand connected with this beautiful creature of the sea, I was once again faced with an overwhelming longing to be free. Straightening up, I watched the ripples settle as he disappeared beneath the surface and we returned back to shore on our rocky boat surrounded by excited tourists who had managed to get a glimpse of Fungi in those few seconds. But as we retraced our journey back down the Dingle Peninsula later that evening, I sensed that life as I knew it was over.

The next day we made our trip back through Ireland to catch the ferry to Holyhead. Later in the evening I stood alone at the back of the boat in the cold night air, watching the lights of Dublin flicker and fade, until eventually they vanished from sight. The stillness of the night settled between us, and with only the blackness of the ocean for company, for the first time in my life I could imagine how it must feel to have a broken heart.

Life was busy with our young family when we returned to Lancashire, but I could not settle. I longed to go back. My husband had a good job in England, so a move to another country was not feasible, and therefore we agreed on a compromise. We decided to visit Ireland again the next summer and to put our house up for sale so that we would move into the countryside. This seemed to be the best solution all round, as there was more than just me to think about in this matter. The sign went up outside the house and I waited patiently for the move to the country. The months passed by slowly, but the house did not sell.

At this point Lee was due to start school in the September, so the chance of moving anywhere before then was almost impossible. I do not remember exactly how I was feeling at this point, but the compulsion to go to Ireland had not gone away. In desperation I asked my husband if I could take the boys back to Ireland and stay with my relatives for the last two months of the summer before Lee started school. He was aware of how much I had loved Ireland, as he too had enjoyed the holiday. He agreed to this arrangement and decided to travel across with us for the first week.

Once more as a family we set off for Ireland. By now we had bought a car and, since my husband cycled to work every day, it was decided that I would keep the car with me in Ireland. With the car packed to the brim, I said goodbye to my parents. I remember my father standing next to me at the back of the car as we said our goodbyes. Taking hold of my shoulders he asked me what it was I was doing. Thinking back, they must have been totally bewildered by it all. I do not remember my reply, but I sometimes wonder what it was.

I never returned to England at the end of summer, and I suppose I never really expected to. The invisible pull that had guided me back across the Irish Sea was far too strong to heed any man-made arguments as to why I should return to England. Even as I write this, I am staggered by how someone so young was able to make this life-changing decision based on a two-week holiday the previous year. Yet that is exactly what I did.

My husband returned to England after the first week and the boys and I settled into our holiday. I managed to find some work locally so as not to be an extra financial strain on my husband. We also found a small cottage to rent nearby, as the boys were full of life and I didn't want them to disturb my relatives. I remember the first day we moved into the cottage with our few belongings. When everyone had waved goodbye and left us alone, I struggled to light my first fire with matches and sticks. After I had settled the boys into their beds, I sat alone in the sitting room with a dubious fire for company. Staring out into the darkness, my father's words came back to haunt me and for the first time since arriving, I too wondered what on earth I was doing.

Over the next few years we commuted between England and Ireland, as our house had still not sold. This may seem an unusual arrangement to some, but since we now both had jobs it worked out quite well. But as time passed we grew further apart until one day I knew in my heart the marriage was over. I do not want to sound harsh or dismissive, but the ending of my marriage is not a story for this book as is still too close to my heart to share. We all know that there are no guarantees in love or life, and the day I walked down the aisle on my father's arm I never expected for one minute that my marriage would end so unexpectedly. Yet it did, and the unusual ending of my marriage had come about from feelings I still neither recognised nor understood.

Each day our lives in Ireland were filled with so many different activities and possibilities that the years swept past in a whirl. Before it seemed possible the boys had moved into their teens and began growing into young men. The time had passed by in a blur of hundreds of thousands of moments that all add up to a lifetime of memories. How could one possibly describe them except to say that in the sense of this world, life had been kind to me.

8

Autumn

*I*t was now four years since I had received the gift voucher. I had used my new abilities in so many different ways, it seemed almost impossible to remember a time when I had been without them. Yet despite all that had happened so far, I sensed that there was more to this unusual gift I now possessed.

Then one sunny afternoon while walking my dogs down a lane we always took, I became aware of a small forest that lay to our left. We had never ventured inside, as it was a forest that was cultivated and it saddened me to think that one day it would all be cut down. I hold a deep respect for trees, conscious of their almost timeless magnificence as they can live for hundreds of years and while understanding the ever-increasing importance of renewable energy, I was reluctant to grow fond of a walk that was destined for destruction.

This day, however, something was different. A strength of energy from within the trees grew to such an extent that I stopped walking altogether to gauge what it was. The urge to go inside became so overwhelming that, ignoring all my previous reservations, I stepped off the path and into the forest.

There was little sunlight beneath the tall trees and it felt cool, damp and a little eerie, but I kept walking further in with my dogs, who were now elated by the scents and sounds of an unexpected new walk. Wandering deeper through the conifers, I became aware of a pulling sensation from the middle of my chest. It felt as if I was being drawn by an invisible magnet and so I followed.

After a few minutes I reached a small clearing filled with broken beams of sunlight. In the middle was a tree that must have seeded itself when the conifers were being planted. I did not recognise what kind of tree it was, as many of its branches were dead and lay on the ground, with the tree itself covered in lichen and moss. Instinctively knowing not to move any closer, I stood admiring the way the sun filtered light through the branches, onto the trunk, creating an effect of warmth and beauty in the middle of a regimented wood.

While standing there, I suddenly realised that I was no longer alone. Through my third eye, I became aware of a massive presence in the clearing. It was that of a young woman, seated, resting with her back against the tree. Looking at her closely, I was struck by her beauty and serenity. Although she made herself visible to me, she appeared oblivious to my presence and was quite content in her own company.

Her energy was new to me. She was not a spirit, but

nor was she an angel. She was dressed in all the hues of autumn, a spectrum of orange, red, gold and brown. Even her dress appeared to be made from the fallen leaves that are characteristic of this beautiful season. What was perhaps most fascinating though, were her eyes and eyelashes. They were exquisite. Her eyes held a liquid-gold light to them, and when she blinked, her eyelashes were very fine, small twigs. She was stunning to gaze upon. I was intrigued, yet was unable to communicate with her, as she continued to ignore me.

I began to feel annoyed.

'Why did you bring me into the forest if you are not going to speak to me?' I demanded to know. 'You would have known that I didn't want to come in here in the first place.'

There was no answer. Then for some reason a wave of loneliness washed over me as I thought of the future of the trees and I began to cry. As my true feelings surfaced, she began to speak, but still without looking at me.

'Try not to think about the future of the trees in that way, but enjoy them while they are still here.'

After she had spoken, unsure of what to do next, I tried asking for her name, but she did not reply. Standing quietly in her company, I attempted to compose myself and gather my thoughts. Deciding to try a different tactic, I asked,

'Do you have a message for me?' Maybe that was why we were now here together. This time her response was immediate:

'You are to write a book.'

I was stunned, completely taken aback by this reply. It was the last thing I had expected her to say, yet at the same time didn't doubt her for a moment. I hastily spoke again, in case she left.

'What sort of book?' I asked.

Again, she answered without hesitation. 'You are to write a book about Mother Earth and all the animals whose voices cannot be heard by humans.'

After giving myself a few minutes for this amazing revelation to sink in, I began to feel frustrated. Considering the ups and downs of the past few years, trying to cope with my psychic abilities as well as carrying on with my day-to-day life, the idea of now writing a book about Mother Earth seemed a bit much.

Along with many other people, I have always been distressed by the continuous destruction of native habitats throughout the world and of the blatant disregard for the protection of vulnerable species. I have a deep respect for nature, but to write a book about it? I stood staring across at her speechless, as panic also began to set in, probably due to the enormity of what she was asking me to do. My mind was already fast-forwarding through images of trying to explain myself to the general public on television. I had seen others attempting do this when talking about angels, noting the underlying sarcasm that sometimes accompanied these interviews. Just the thought of having to do something similar was too unbearable to even contemplate. Could you imagine trying to explain my story? No way was I getting involved in this. I was definitely the wrong person for the task. Forgetting all about speaking to her through telepathy in case anyone else came into the wood, I shouted across the clearing to her.

'I won't do it. Go and find somebody else!' This outburst was met with more silence, so I tried again.

'How can I possibly help save Mother Earth or protect the animals of the world? You are being ridiculous. No one would listen to me. Then added as an afterthought, 'Why can't you all just leave me alone?'

Her response to this outburst only seemed to seal my fate, as, finally, she turned to look at me directly and I quailed under the intensity of her gaze. With eyes resembling rivers of pure gold, she answered. 'You are Thor Shahina. You will become a voice for nature, helping to save hundreds of thousands of plants and animals. Go home and begin to write.'

With a heavy heart, I turned to leave the forest, wishing I had not spoken to her at all. Now it seemed I even had a name. Unable to resist, I glanced back to see if she was still there and she was, in exactly the same position. Once again this confirmed that she wasn't an angel I could associate with, as they never stay once a message is relayed. Whoever or whatever she was, she was extremely powerful and influential. I trudged home with my dogs, almost weeping in misery at the latest outcome from my association with celestial beings. I felt that this request was going one step too far, not to mention the fact that I had absolutely no idea how to write a book.

Returning home I found Thomas watching television and I had an idea. In the vain hope that the whole episode had been a figment of my imagination, I asked him if he would mind coming into the forest to look at some energy I had seen there, but didn't recognise. Nothing more was said about the incident in case it influenced his answer. As always, he agreed without hesitation.

We were soon retracing my steps to the clearing, where we then stood together in silence. We were there for so long, in fact, that I began to get worried. 'Can you see anything?' I asked tentatively, sincerely hoping he would say no, although I could still see the presence clearly.

More agonizing moments of silence passed before he answered.

'Well, there's a large amount of energy adjacent to the tree in the clearing in front of us ... but it has no definite shape'.

Surprised that he wasn't able to see the young girl as I could, I recounted everything I had seen and heard, hoping he would laugh out loud and say how ridiculous I was becoming. But he too turned to look directly at me and said, 'Well what are you waiting for? Write it.'

In spite of myself I was intrigued by the name 'Thor Shahina'. What could it mean? The next day I decided to see if it could be translated into the English language and started searching online. It didn't take long to find either name. Thor is of course known from Norse mythology as the hammer-wielding god. He was associated with thunder, lightning, storms, oak trees, strength, the protection of mankind, and also hallowing, healing and fertility! Quite a god! My biggest surprise came though from finding an ancient Arabic name 'Shahina' translated as 'Princess'.

I returned many times to the tree in the wood and the girl. She never gave me any name, but I came to think of her as 'Autumn'. Often, when upset or worried, I almost instinctively turned beneath the trees to find her. On reaching the tree I would run my hands along its cool branches, resting my face against the soft moss or sit on a low bough. In the silence that surrounded us I would tell her of the troubles that were impossible to share with others. The extent of my psychic abilities. The loneliness they have created within my life as, apart from my sons, I knew of no one like myself with whom to share them; and the inability to understand what she was now asking me to do. As always, she was there to listen, but when I rose to leave, whatever my reasons were for going to see her, the words 'write the book', were echoing through the trees.

After a few months, it seemed obvious that I was going to have to give some serious thought to this 'book'. Being familar with academic writing would surely seem an advantage, but unlike theoretical work in a university, there was no instant access to a celestial library. I only had my own experiences to rely on which seemed neither relevant, nor appropriate. Slightly perplexed, I thought it might be a good idea to first explore the world of publishing.

After an initial search on the internet, I found what seemed to be a suitable publisher in London and rang them up. Politely, but firmly, I was told to go and buy the Writers' and Artists' Yearbook to understand how to approach a publishing company properly. Suitably chastised, I visited the local bookshop the following day to purchase my copy. On opening the door, a cheery bell rang out heralding my arrival. After exchanging pleasantries with the shop assistant, I browsed around while she went in search of a copy. On her return, I was shocked to see the book in her hands. It looked about the size of the Holy Bible. 'Are you sure that's the right book?' I blurted out before I could help myself.

One withering glance was enough for me to know that it was and in a daze I left the shop with the book tucked under my arm. This time it felt as if the bell on the door had a slightly mocking sound to it as I left.

The next three months were spent trying to make some sense of the publishing world, including the correct way to approach publishers. I became somewhat lost amid a world of introductory letters, personal bios, synopses, sample chapters and 'writer's block'. Eventually acknowledging that one does not simply sit down and write a book, I decided to take part in a book-writing course in London that I had seen advertised online. Not wishing to go alone, Thomas, who was still living at home at this point, was invited along. Seizing the chance of an all expenses paid trip to London, he accompanied me on my travels and we set off the following week.

The Houses of Parliament, London

It was a particularly hot week in England, and as the course finished quite early on the last day, we decided to make use of the fine weather and met up to fit in a small amount of sightseeing. We both found London to be a fabulous city that felt vibrantly alive. We joined a boat trip up the River Thames, entertained by a hilarious commentary from the guide on board, who recounted London's somewhat dubious past.

We then decided to visit Westminster Abbey. Unfortunately as it was now nearly five o'clock it had closed for the day. We strolled along the roadside in the beautiful sunshine debating what to do instead. Thomas stopped for a few minutes to get tissues from his bag, while I kept slowly walking along the path on the opposite side of the road from the Houses of Parliament. Absentmindedly gazing at the building, I became aware of how beautiful it was and continued admiring it until I reached the Sovereign Entrance. This part of the building looked particularly majestic and I sat on a small wall to admire it properly, while waiting for Thomas to catch up.

After a few moments I felt a strong urge to look behind. It felt as though someone was staring at me. Glancing back, no-one was there. Instead there was another building, much smaller than The Houses of Parliament, directly behind me. Feeling somewhat drawn to it, I walked over to read the information plaque about its history. It was called the Jewel Tower and while I stood there reading, a peaceful energy began swirling all around me, even though I was on the side of a very busy road. Not sure what was happening, yet knowing it was related to the Jewel Tower, I decided to see if it was possible to go inside. Unfortunately, this too was now closed. Thomas had re-joined me at this stage and I explained what I had felt and my disappointment at not being able to go inside.

We pondered what to do for a moment, until I felt a sudden urge to walk around to the back of the tower. The tower is set on a very small site, with a dry moat running round it, making it possible to walk all around. Strolling over to a bench at the back, I sat down while Thomas wandered off. There was nothing particular to see behind the tower, but I could still feel the strong yet peaceful energy everywhere and was becoming very curious as to what it was. Getting up, I felt an urge to move in a certain direction, similar to when I had first met Autumn in the forest. Quite abruptly, I stopped near a small tree, knowing that I was now standing in exactly the right place, although uncertain of what was going to happen next. Patiently waiting, I was unaware of the world around me.

Did a spirit want to make contact with me? Nothing stirred, so I tried to gauge the situation through my third eye. All was still. Unsure of what to do next, I turned back to face the Jewel Tower to find it bathed in brilliant white light. The light was so intense that I couldn't see the tower at all. Within the light there was a figure, but it was impossible to distinguish it clearly. Unlike Autumn in the forest, this presence spoke to me without hesitation and the message was very clear and direct. I was told that angels are just as beautiful as the Sovereign Entrance of The Houses of Parliament that I had been admiring earlier and that through my book, I must translate messages of love from the angelic realm. These messages would give people an opportunity to understand the beauty of their realm, as clearly as they are able to understand visual beauty in this world, just as I had. Through my words, others could then learn to love everyone and everything from the heart again, as this is the hardest test for us all.

The words were simple, yet profound in meaning, and the tremendous responsibility that was being bestowed upon me did not go unnoticed. The message was not referring to loving people that we already know and care for, as that was far too obvious. It meant everyone and everything that we came into contact with, giving all living things the respect and dignity they rightly deserve. It was not a request, nor was it an order, yet its importance was crystal-clear.

Shocked by such a task and forgetting people might hear, instinctively stretching out my hand I called out, 'Please don't go. Stay and help me to do this, please.' Yet the light only brightened slightly for a split second and then it was gone.

9

Guardian Angels

The thought that a guardian angel may be standing close beside me was not something I had ever dwelt on to any great extent. Perhaps, like many others, it was simply because I had never been able to see them with my physical eye. Now, though, I very much wanted to see one appear. I had two difficult pieces of work to write, one for Autumn in regard to nature; and another for the angels about love. Both of these subjects are complex issues and I longed for some guidance or reassurance that celestial beings were watching over me while I attempted to do this. Even a feather falling to the ground while walking through the fields would have sufficed at this point, but none floated down.

People with the gift of clairvoyance often tell me that I am surrounded by large angels, protecting me at all times. While I find this somewhat reassuring I often wonder why, if there are so many, some of them don't clearly guide me as they had done with Joan of Arc? It felt as if I was involved in some kind of celestial guessing game. On top of this, I was not too sure how I felt about my every move being watched day and night. Being told years ago that spirits are very discreet and know when to make themselves scarce, I rather hoped the same applied to celestial beings. This is not so certain, as Thomas once told me that he could see seven guides that surrounded his bed each night. He said that when he switched off the bedroom light and got into bed, he could see them clearly, being able to describe their appearance to me in great detail. Together we spent quite some time trying to figure out what they were all for but to no avail. He seems totally unconcerned by so many watching him as he sleeps and so I have valiantly tried to follow his example.

Have you ever felt the presence of a guardian angel by your side? A sense of calm and comfort surrounding you in an unexpected moment, or perhaps a helping hand when you least expected it? Maybe you didn't realise angels were there, guiding you through a difficult situation, one that seemed almost too impossible to bear.

We become so caught up within a crisis, that we often take little heed of an unexpected change of events, later putting it down to good luck or fate, yet these situations are often watched over by angels. They have an ability to intervene in the physical world in the most amazing ways, and always for the good. I have known angels do this many times, although I do not know why they choose to help some people and not others. I have also witnessed them save lives. Each time they arrive as silently as they leave, without prompting or prior notice and I thought I might share some of these stories with you.

Signs from above

At the age of seven or eight although I don't remember having many toys, the bedroom I shared with my sister was awash with plants of every description, shape and size, which I cared for lovingly. These plants were my pride and joy. I suppose one could call this fascination a hobby and that was certainly how I saw it at the time. But now I know there was much more to this bond with nature as it was through these plants that I first felt the presence of an angel. Although I had no understanding of what was happening at the time, an angel came to comfort me in a moment of great distress and it is the clarity with which I remember the incident, that made it obvious something very unusual happened.

It began one summer's evening while being put to bed. My grandfather was ill in hospital with cancer at the time, but being so young I had no understanding of this illness nor the concept of death. Yet as my mother said my prayers, I suddenly knew he was going to die. I have no idea where this thought came from, but recall it vividly. I began to cry bitterly, knowing I would never sit on the floor beside his chair again while he gently stroked my hair. My mother could not console me, so my sister was sent to fetch my father. Crying into my pillow, I longed to be near Grandad one last time to tell him how much I loved him. My mother left the room for a few moments and I stared sightlessly at my beloved plants through a veil of tears. Suddenly a sense of stillness began to settle in the room. I lay motionless, aware that I was no longer alone. Someone was standing beside me trying to comfort me. I couldn't see anything, but could feel an indescribable sense of peace and the tears dried on my face where they lay. This sensation is now instantly recognisable as being identical to that of a heartlink, meaning an angel was nearby. My breathing settled as I lay in the angel's calm energy and a warmth stole around my body, almost like a hug. I definitely felt as though I was being embraced. When my father came into the room I had settled considerably, although I never told him what had happened. Lulled by the unexpected comfort yet still not understanding it, I fell into a deep sleep while both my father and an angel watched over me.

An unexpected helping hand

One time an angel came to my aid in my twenties and it was quite dramatic. It was a lovely summer's afternoon I was walking home with my two young sons after visiting my parents. At that time we had no car, and 'double buggies' were a thing of the future. I used an old-style *Silver Cross* pram to transport my two sons, who were both under three years of age. These prams were quite large, with a carriage-style body and four large wheels. They were designed for one child, but another seat could be added across the body of the pram for a toddler to sit on.

It was an impressive object, but quite heavy to push!

On this particular day, after picking up some groceries, I decided to stop at a little park adjacent to the road we were walking along. It was so warm that I thought the boys might enjoy playing in the sunshine. This park was very familiar, as I had spent many hours in it as a teenager, playing tennis. The courts were no longer in use, but the flowerbeds were still well tended, and the heady scent of the roses seemed to call to me from the dusty road above. Being on a much lower level than the main road, I had to guide the pram down a steep incline to reach the gardens. I managed it without any great difficulty and the boys were soon enjoying toddling and crawling amongst the flowerbeds and, by pure chance, we had the place to ourselves.

After about half an hour it was time to be on our way. I strapped the boys back onto the pram and we set off up another path that would lead us to the main road again. Climbing the lane, for the first time I noticed the weight of the pram. This didn't unduly bother me until, on turning a slight curve, I realised that the weight was starting to bear back on me. Slightly alarmed, my walking slowed to a crawl. I was aware that we were now surrounded by trees on both sides making our predicament invisible to anyone on the road above and, glancing back, I could see there was still no-one in the park to call for help. Trying not to panic my pace came to a complete stop. The handle of the pram was now wedged firmly against my stomach with the weight of two children and a full tray of shopping now bearing down heavily against me. It was an effort not to step backwards. I was unable to reach for the brakes with my foot as to do so would have added too much pressure to my other leg and I could not take a hand off the handlebar either. In those few seconds the seriousness of the situation struck me like a knife through my heart. I gazed at my two sons, who up to this point had been oblivious to any danger. Then Lee caught my eye, and even though he was only three years old, I knew he realised something was wrong. The next minute, and the results of it, were very soon going to be out of my control, as my legs began to tremble.

From out of nowhere, a hand appeared on the handlebar beside me to my right. For a couple of seconds I stared down at it stupidly, confused as to where it had come from, then, glancing up, I saw a man standing beside me. Smiling down he said, 'It looks like the path is a bit steeper than you thought and that you could do with a little help.'

I was so shaken by my predicament that I don't remember what I murmured back, but my relief must have been palpable and I remember his words clearly. His strength took over the weight of the pram and we soon reached the top of the path, re-joining the busy road. It is often at moments such as this, that mere words seem totally inadequate to thank someone. What could have happened had he not appeared when he did was not worth thinking about. I turned to thank him, but he was gone. Stunned, I looked all around me, but he had simply vanished. I could see the road clearly both ways as it was a straight stretch, but he wasn't there. He was also not on the path we had just travelled up. Puzzled and feeling slightly sick from my ordeal, I set off home again.

I have revisited this incident in my mind many times over the years and have always had to concede that there was no explanation for the appearance or disappearance of this man. He could not have seen our dilemma from the road above and if he had, he would have reached us by coming down the lane and I knew there was no way he had followed me up. It is said that guardian angels can miraculously appear in a physical form, although it is extremely rare. I believe that for the boys and myself, this was one of these times.

The thought that an angel came to my aid at a time of distress has never failed to fill me with wonder and I often wish that I could see him one more time. Have there been thousands of other times when angels make this remarkable transition into our world to save lives or comfort us? I believe this to be very likely and was reminded of how many people long for 'a sign from above'.

For some people, the simple notion of a white feather drifting down from the sky is enough proof from the heavens that they are not alone. Indeed, this simple representation of heaven has brought great comfort to many individuals in difficult times. A symbol that verifies the belief that there is a world beyond our own, associated with paradise, a place many people believe they will see when they die and be reunited with their loved ones. We are taught that paradise is free from the human experience of pain, grief, torment, anguish, heartache and sorrow, yet there are some who do not believe that such a place could possibly exist, finding it simpler to believe in nothing at all. However, many others the whole world over, although challenged by arguments that seek to question or ridicule a world that cannot be proven, have kept their faith. They firmly believe in a place unseen to the human eye that is governed by a divine presence, founded in love. A realm that coexists, with our own, that can somehow reach us in times of trouble, reassuring us that we are being watched over. And it does not seem unrealistic to accept that some of these people long for a 'sign', to reassure them that it truly exists.

I have two very clear recollections when I have glimpsed some understanding of the significance of a 'sign from above'. One, when someone was desperately seeking a sign but none was forthcoming and another, when a person was completely unaware that they were actually receiving one.

Some things are best left unsaid

Medjugorje is famous the world over for the sightings of Mary, the Mother of Jesus allegedly seen by six young children thirty-two years ago on a hillside whilst out playing. Since that day Mary still visits these individuals, now adults, with messages to pass on to the world.

Messages of love and compassion and a plea for everyone to turn back to God. I had always been slightly intrigued by the events that unfolded in the small village, and it seems that I was not alone, as approximately 40 million people of all different faiths and religions have travelled across the world to be there. While holidaying in Croatia with Thomas, we decided to cross the border into Bosnia and take the trip to see Medjugorje for ourselves.

We arrived into the town by bus, not really knowing what to expect. As soon as we alighted, we were greeted by an array of stalls on the streets selling memorabilia in recognition of the apparitions of Mary. We browsed around a couple, but soon realised that many of them were selling very similar products. After purchasing a few medallions for family members back home, we sat in a cafe discussing what we might do next. Our time was limited before the return journey on the bus. We already knew that we would not have time to visit both the church, where the messages were relayed, and Apparition Hill, where Mary first appeared to the children.

After much deliberation, we decided that we would both prefer to stay out in the sunshine and visit the site where Mary had appeared and we set off to find the small goats' path that snaked up to the site. It was a beautiful summer's day, which, along with bringing out hordes of people, had also attracted various species of insects neither of us had ever seen before. I tend to get bitten very easily, so we paused at the bottom of the track so that I could put on my insect repellent.

Before leaving Ireland I had purchased an organic spray made from various flowers which actually smelt really nice. With my task complete and smelling beautifully, I firmly pulled on my big straw hat to protect my face and neck from the increasingly hot sun and we set off on the path that millions of others had trodden before us. It was quite tricky to negotiate a goat path in summer sandals. As well as being steep, there were a lot of loose stones underfoot and my full attention was soon caught up with the task of not twisting my ankle. Thomas on the other hand was in his element, bounding ahead with a new camera taking pictures of the assortment of large colourful insects. It did not take long for the midday heat to take its toll, slowing me down considerably and I was soon lagging far behind. I stopped for a rest at one of the stations of the cross on the route. While pausing to cool down, a middle-aged couple were approaching me from further down the path and I set off up the hill again keeping slightly ahead. They were close enough for me to hear their conversation and, in spite of myself, it caught my attention. The lady had caught the scent of my spray and was remarking on it to her partner. Glancing back, I could see that they had stopped walking so she could smell the air properly. Thomas was sitting waiting on a low stone wall just ahead and as I caught up to him, we fell back into step together. Behind us we could hear the lady repeatedly commenting on the scent. Suddenly she exclaimed quite loudly that she believed that it was a sign from Mary that she was present on their ascent to the apparition site. I was slightly taken aback that she thought my spray may be a sign from heaven, although on reflection, it did not seem unreasonable to hope that here, more than anywhere else in the world, there might be the chance of 'sensing' a heavenly presence. I turned to Thomas whispering that now might be a good time to let her know what it actually was. After a pause he said perhaps it may be better not to, leaving her to believe that in this moment Mary was indeed present. Silently we made our way to the statue which marks the place where Our Lady first appeared to the children. As we joined crowds of people quietly praying at her feet and sensed an air of great calm, I had to agree with my son that some things are best left unsaid.

Feathers on the ground

My last story takes us to a beautiful spot called Witch Wood in Lytham in Lancashire. Once while visiting a friend who lived there, I decided to take my dogs for a walk in these woods alone. Soon after stepping off a busy roadside, I paused under a canopy of trees stretching far above into a beautiful blue sky. The ground below was ablaze with a carpet of bluebells, and it seemed as though I had stepped into some kind of heaven on earth.

Finding a quiet bench to sit on, I basked in the silence, enjoying the solitude. Then from a distance I became aware of two women chatting together who I could just see through the trees. They appeared to know each other well by the sound of their voices. Then one of them began to cry. The other woman rushed to hold her in her arms. I couldn't hear what was being said, but in spite of myself I was curious. Through telepathy I tried to gauge the energy of the situation and quickly realised that the sobbing woman had recently lost her husband after a long illness and was struggling with her grief. She had decided to visit the woods as it was a place much loved by them both, in the hope of regaining a sense of being close to him. By her obvious distressed state, the trip had not turned out as she had hoped.

Glancing down at my dogs quietly relaxing in the sun, I almost willed them to remain silent so that we would not be spotted. I did not know what to do next, or how much longer the dogs would stay still. Something needed to be done. For some reason I thought of my father. I heard his voice saying, 'Well, what are you waiting for? Do something.'

Knowing exactly what he meant, I immediately began a heartlink to the angels, asking for some sense of comfort be given to the woman before me.

Within seconds, the same change in energy that I had noticed in the Sistine Chapel in Rome began to descend into the woods. It seemed as if the air around the three of us was pushed apart, almost akin to opening a set of curtains in the morning, allowing another, much more powerful energy through. Within this energy there was an enormous angel who enfolded the two women within her wings. From where I sat, it looked as if the scene was being captured within a huge and impenetrable bubble of light. As the energy emanating from the angel penetrated the grieving woman's aura, her sobbing subsided.

Oblivious to my presence, the two women chatted quietly and then turned to leave, this time in the same direction. Once more alone, I pondered on the scene that had just unfolded before me. Neither of the women had any idea what had just taken place, yet I knew that an incredibly powerful angel had just stepped forward to offer comfort and support. There were no signs left to show that an angel had been present – no snow-white feathers on the ground to take home as a reminder. But I believe the heavens had been one step ahead of all of us that day, with feathers already lying in place. Her friend out for a walk and myself, sat on the bench, ready for her visit.

10

Flowers & Fairies

Looking back on the many times I have made contact with spirits, it seems there is much to thank them for. Quite unintentionally they helped me understand how incredible being alive actually is. It is staggering how many emotions can be caught up within the spirit world, as the deceased become trapped within the various levels of ascension after leaving the physical plane. This ascension is very much dependent on how much the spirit is still attached to the whole process of being alive, or whether they are aware that they have died at all. I find it quite humbling that they are willing to share their stories with me, as I am a complete stranger and many of their tales are quite tragic and personal.

The reason many souls do not move on seems to be related to lingering feelings of anger, frustration, resentment, injustice or worry. This confusion, more often than not influenced by matters of the heart, had me reassessing my own life. It did not take long to decide that I had no desire to be caught up in a similar state of limbo, trapped between two worlds. Also the chance of there being an individual, such as myself, on hand to help with a smoother ascension, if required, seemed somewhat slim.

But how does one protect oneself from such an outcome? Books on the topic are not exactly readily available. Determined to persevere though, I devised my own technique. The first and most obvious question I asked myself was, 'Am I happy?' This answer proved to be dependent on various complicated tangents, usually involving other people. Therefore to address the question honestly and using stories from my mentors of the past to guide me, I began examining every aspect of my life.

Sitting alone quietly, I brought to mind relationships or situations that might be bothering me and there seemed to be quite a few! Holding any thoughts or feelings that came to mind, I began to note where these situations were harboured in my physical body. An unexplained stiff neck, the niggling backache, a strange stabbing pain in my right side in times of stress, tension headaches, restless nights, feelings of unease, fear and tingles of apprehension. God, I was a mess, influenced by so many outside factors! Listening to my body as never before, I visualised releasing toxic situations from my life once and for all and the results were simply incredible. Feelings of complete calm and peace would replace the confusion and anxiety that had been there before. It was astonishing how quickly the body could resolve an underlying issue once it had been acknowledged and the decision was finally made to let it go. The most important part of the technique was definitely the willingness 'to let go'. This interesting process quickly put in place a new way of thinking, helping me to re-evaluate the priorities in my life enormously, resulting in many adjustments as to how I went about my day, how my time was delegated and who it was spent with.

Until the present of the gift voucher, I had been caught up in a day filled with endless deadlines to be met. Deadlines that seemed to drain me emotionally, physically and financially. Not only that, but they always seemed to be for someone else's benefit and never my own. I had also been making the mistake of eating on the go, drinking too many caffeinated drinks and driving faster than I should when we were late. Now I realised that neither my life nor anyone else's would end if we were five minutes late for work, school, a dentist or doctor's appointment or any other seemingly pressing engagement.

So I started to find moments in the day to do things I wanted to do, rather than what had to be done and it took a while to discover what they actually were. That is not to say I became a self-absorbed, selfish person, in fact the opposite was usually the case. Whereas before, I might have been queuing with my groceries at a checkout tapping my foot impatiently, counting the seconds until being served, this became the perfect moment to be pleasant to someone standing beside me. Therefore what had once appeared to be an irritating inconvenience and a complete waste of my time, now became a way of perhaps adding some colour and sparkle to both my day and that of another.

As I strove to achieve this new way of living, I began to feel more relaxed and content. I started to enjoy my own company and no longer had an interest in the many forms of stimuli that assault our senses on a daily basis, namely: mindless television, negative news, gossip columns or magazines, to name but a few. These only seek to cloud our minds and hearts with stories or facts which are far beyond the reach of our own worlds and ultimately of little use to our daily lives. Why should I watch or read something that might bring me down or upset me? It made no sense at all. How was I ever going to feel good about myself if I bombarded myself with negativity. I have always hated violence of any sort and have never really understood why so many TV programmes portray it as entertainment. How as a society do we condone this style of 'enlightenment'? I felt an urge to escape from the world of technology and rediscover the world around me. To expand on how this was initially achieved, there is one particular early memory that best describes what I am trying to convey.

One beautiful summer's morning early in June while driving into the city for a meeting, I had a sudden impulse to stop the car and take a walk beside a river that could be seen meandering beside the road. There was half an hour to spare and I decided that this was how I was going to use it, rather than stopping to pick up a coffee. I had passed the river countless times on journeys throughout the years without giving it more than a passing glance, but today was different. Finding a gateway to park the car safely, I was soon walking through long grass and scrambling among some particularly unfriendly brambles to reach the river. Content, although somewhat bloodied, I strolled alongside the meandering bank, under a beautiful blue sky wondering why I had never done this before. The path followed a gentle bend of the river and I came across a scene that took my breath away. This part of the water was slow moving and covered in a carpet of white flowers. The flowers were so numerous, that it was difficult to spot the sparkling river beneath. Swimming through this dense carpet of flowers were two swans lost in each other's company and oblivious to mine. They swam so closely beside each other, almost entwined, that it was difficult to distinguish one from the other and it looked as if they were moving as one. The sun had transformed the white brilliance of their feathers and that of the flowers into an almost impossible beauty and I hardly dared to breathe in case they were disturbed.

Entranced by the unexpectedness of what I had chanced upon, I stood watching, motionless, knowing that wild swans are very easily disturbed and always alert to danger. As they took turns, bending their necks elegantly to drink from the water, it looked like they were performing a very intimate dance. I began to back away to a place where they wouldn't be able to see me and then turning, retraced my steps back to the car deep in thought.

The sights, smells and sounds of that scene have remained with me ever since and are as crystal clear as the first moment they were experienced. Although it is hard to recall the exact moment when it happened, it feels as though it was after witnessing this scene that the love of nature which had come so naturally to me as a child, was rekindled.

As if wakened from a deep unconscious sleep by the experiences of these exhilarating moments, I wanted to spend as much time as possible in nature. Whereas before, walking my dogs after work had felt somewhat of a chore, I was now impatient for my workday to end, longing for the moment when I could shrug off life and pull on my wellies, free at last to mingle with nature as we ambled down country lanes, through woods and along river banks. Whether turning to 'Autumn' for solace, or sitting quietly beside a babbling brook or rushing river, I grew ever more accustomed to the rhythm of nature, so easily overlooked in the modern world.

Over time and by sitting quietly in the meadow with some tattered nature books and an old pair of binoculars from my father, hours were spent alone lost in thought, attempting to learn about this new world around me. It seemed beyond belief that twenty-four years of my life had been spent in an academic setting, yet I knew so little about what surrounded me in the natural world. Over time I began to recognise the many species of birds, animals, insects, flowers and trees. This was no mean feat and it took years to learn not only the names of all the different species, but also their sounds, scents or appearance. There was so much to admire; the robin fiercely defending his one-acre territory with his melodious song, which until this time, I had ridiculously thought was for our pleasure. The tiny wren warbling the sweetest of songs, a song thrush singing its crystal clear notes across the still evening skies; the harsh call of an elusive jay, the lonesome cry of a solitary buzzard soaring high above, a family of otters catching breakfast in the river or foxes playing in a field. Where does one stop?

My favourite pastime grew to become a part of nature's transition from day into night. Those few minutes when the activities of the day cease, allowing the stillness of the night to begin. Sitting on our old hammock from where a view of the sky is endless, I was free to watch the daily phenomena, when the sky lost the light from the last rays of the sun, giving way to the shimmering stars in a velvety darkness.

Within this silence I was able to watch the bats and moths begin their game of 'catch' and, if very lucky, would hear the swoosh of wings as an owl flew overhead in search of its first meal. The thought of the mere chance of this sight, rarely seen now, held my attention more than any television, radio, book or conversation could have ever done. And it was while attempting to understand nature in this way that I became aware of a very different sound.

I first sensed it while walking through a field with the dogs. Within the silence around me, I could clearly hear movement. It was as though millions of atoms were darting about in different directions, sometimes passing each other by, and sometimes colliding. Stopping to listen carefully, I realised it was a sound within the sound of silence, so elusive that it could easily be missed. A vibrational communication between all living things. I have heard of people who thought trees could communicate with each other and had simply dismissed this as a rather romantic notion. Yet here I was listening to that exact sound, but it was not just between the trees, it was between every living thing, but what was it saying? I wanted to know and it was while attempting to understand nature in this way, that I began to 'see' clearly, just like Thomas, with my physical eye.

The first time this happened was while relaxing in the garden watching a butterfly resting on a dandelion. After consulting my father's butterfly book, it was easily recognisable as a red admiral and this one seemed to be enjoying a rare treat in Ireland, that of a hot summer's afternoon. Happily settled with its wings opened out fully to soak up the intense rays of the sun, it was easy to observe it closely and I couldn't help but admire its beauty.

As we shared this quiet moment together, a band of coloured light around its wings became visible. It was about half an inch wide and softly coloured in shades of blue and pink. Suddenly the butterfly closed its wings tightly shut. Fascinated, I watched, wondering if I would see the aura again. It began opening and closing its wings repeatedly and each time the same thing was visible, an aura surrounding the wings every time they were down.

This went on for at least another ten minutes while it rested, oblivious to its captivated audience. Eventually it flew away and I was glad that it had stayed the length of time it did, as initially when the aura was visible I thought it must surely be a figment of my imagination.

The second time an aura of an animal was visible to me was while hanging the washing out on the line one sunny morning. Reaching up to the line with a mouth full of pegs, something caught my eye in the sky. High above, a buzzard was circling overhead. There was nothing unusual about this sight as they were nesting nearby. What held my attention this time was a flock of other birds following it. Something I had never seen before. Curious, I paused in my task to continue watching. Perhaps the buzzard was teaching its young the complicated aerodynamics of flying, something I enjoyed watching the swallows do each summer: practising manoeuvres, essential for catching insects in flight and ultimately for survival. I wasn't sure if this was what was happening now though, as the birds were too high in the sky to see them clearly.

Then I saw something unusual. As the buzzard circled, it left a trail of green mist behind it, and it was within this trail that the other birds were flying, weaving in and out of it as they flew. This had my full attention. What were they doing? Is this how birds learn to fly, gliding through an aura streaming from the parent bird? What a fascinating thought. I wanted to run inside for my binoculars to get a closer look, or ring my neighbour to come and watch this spectacle with me, but I didn't want to lose sight of the birds either. All of a sudden the birds behind the buzzard stopped swooping in and out of the green trail and flew down to a lower level and I was taken aback to see that they were crows. What had they been doing? Why had they been enjoying the energy of a buzzard, one of their arch enemies and more importantly, why had he allowed them to do it?

Whatever the reason had been, what could no longer be denied was that at long last, I could see energy rather than just perceive it. Enchanted by these experiences and by this new ability, I went back into the house with an empty washing basket and a light heart.

This was the first of many occasions when auras that exist within nature became visible to me and soon after I began to see orbs.

Orbs

Whereas auras outline the appearance of an animal or plant, orbs are sudden bright flashes of beautifully coloured sparkling light. I do not have to concentrate on anything in particular to see them, or consciously go looking for them; they just flash intermittently around me throughout the day. They can appear anywhere and at any time, but especially at home, around people I love, or while out walking in nature. They sparkle as the twinkling stars in the night sky do, but rather than being just white, they can be multicoloured, orange, blue, yellow, pink, or green to name but a few.

Sometimes they flash for only a split second, but can also linger for a few moments and when this happens, people around me are able to observe them too. They can vary in size, with the smallest being probably about the size of a pea, to the largest I have seen being a brilliant bright orange, about the size of a football. I remember being with my Dad on this occasion and we both noticed it at the same time. Dad said that he had never seen anything like it before and, like myself, was baffled as to what it could be. While orbs usually flash singularly like this, on occasion they can be seen in small groups that twinkle together, reminding me of sparklers that children hold at bonfires.

Orbs always appear in calm, relaxed moments of the day and this could well be why I mainly see them in my home where I probably relax the most. As they flash around people I am chatting to they can be very distracting! Animals can see orbs too and our old cat used to spend hours sitting on my bed watching them. She saw far more than any of us have ever seen, constantly turning her head. I'm not sure if she was following their movement, or just that there were so many that she was glancing around to see them all. One day, she even tried to catch one above the headboard by swiping at it with her paw.

My sons and I had always presumed that if I was ever going to see anything with my physical eye, it would either be a spirit or an angel. Yet to this day this has never been the case. Knowing so little about auras and orbs prompted me to consider learning a little more about them. I had already become slightly curious following an incident that had taken place at work.

One day, a girl of about twelve years of age said how she loved coming to see me. Surprised by this announcement, although delighted of course, I enquired as to why. She replied by saying that each time she looked at me, she could see a beautiful orange and yellow glow all around my head and shoulders. Astonished at how clearly she seemed to be able to both see and speak about this, I asked her if it bothered her.

'No,' she replied smiling across at me, 'It makes me feel really happy.'

The simplicity of her answer was touching. Therefore the following month I booked a place to join an aura and chakra workshop being held in the nearby city.

Auras and chakras

The workshop was really enjoyable and it was nice to spend a day in the company of like-minded people. It made me realise how long it had been since I had done anything of this kind and of how I seemed to be unconsciously avoiding it. Feeling slightly uncomfortable for acknowledging such a fact, I made a determined effort to listen carefully throughout the whole morning while auras were explained to us.

Auras are quite complicated to understand, simply

because they are forever changing colour depending on your mood, what you are doing or what you are experiencing. These different colours are associated with many different emotional states, all of which are impossible to list.

Needless to say, everyone became curious as to whether we would be able to see each other's and what colour they might be. The facilitator suggested that we took it in turns to stand against a white painted wall in the room, where we might be able to see the auras more clearly. Eager to begin, one by one we began standing perfectly still against the white backdrop while everybody tried to distinguish some kind of coloured aura. When it came to be my turn to stand in front of the wall something very interesting happened, which no-one other than the facilitator and myself noticed. As the group of people stared around my head, an enormous celestial male figure appeared to my right. Distracted from the exercise by his arrival, I tried to gauge his purpose through my third eye. All of a sudden, he stepped out in front of me, totally blocking my energy from being seen by anyone. After a few more minutes of silence, everyone agreed that they couldn't see any aura around me and probably deemed me to be a very boring individual. When they said this, laughingly, I explained what had happened and the facilitator smiled, saying that she too had watched the male angel step forward.

Because of this incident I often wonder whether auras are not really intended for other people to gaze upon, although there are, of course, many people who can see them. It also made me realise that while these people have a fascination with the elusive, unknown, and sometimes inexplicable vibration of spirit and angel worlds, we have a fabulous vibrational energy all of our own. Not only that, but one that can give us an insight to our overall well-being. I believe the energy contained within our aura is as individual to each of us as a fingerprint. This energy can be so vibrant that sometimes, such as the time when the girl could see mine, they extend outside our bodies. Either because our auras are healthy and vivid, or because an individual is feeling a strong emotion, it is possible for some people to see this clearly. I could be wrong of course, but this is how I imagine it to be.

After a very interesting morning exploring the world of auras, the afternoon turned to the subject of chakras. I soon discovered that my general lack of understanding of auric energy was closely followed by an even greater lack of familiarity with the term 'chakra'.

Chakras

The word chakra comes from an ancient language known as Sanskrit, translating into English as 'spinning wheel' or 'circle'. Chakras are circles of energy spinning within us that attempt to keep our soul and spirit in balance, while we attempt to negotiate the physical world. Chakras reside within our physical bodies, undetectable by most modern medicine and are therefore non-existent to many individuals.

There are many chakra points, but most people are familiar with seven, the crown, brow, throat, heart, solar plexus, sacral and base chakra. These seven points contained within our body could be described as being the essence of who we really are and are vital to our health. They run straight down the middle of the body in a vertical line from the crown on the top of our head to the base, at the seat of our spine, all containing separate centres of energy which radiate light. They are independent of each other and had, unbeknownst to me, been visible to me for quite some time, I just hadn't known what they were.

In 2010 I had decided to try to set some time aside again for healing work, using the I.E.T.® techniques I learnt with Gretta, but now when doing it I began to see spinning wheels of coloured light. They were different from anything that had been explained so far, and were not how celestial energy appears to me. These circles swirled in a clockwise direction, or in some cases did not move at all.

To see them clearly I simply relaxed my eyes and used my third eye to 'look' at a person. By doing this, the person seemed to lose their solid physical appearance, softening into pure energy, which looked a bit like candy floss. Within this softened energy, I could clearly see seven circles, spinning like wheels. They all have different colours, often shining with different intensities. This meant that while some resembled bright sparkling colours, others appeared stagnant and grey, or at the very least, sluggish and 'heavy'. I know the individual chakra are all known by specific colours and that these reflect the different emotions related to the experience of being human. As with the many different angelic names I never trouble myself too much with this concept, but simply observe the energy around each chakra point.

The best way to describe how I see them is to compare them to a rainbow in the sky. Depending on weather conditions, we all know that rainbows can be either vividly colourful and quite spectacular, or appear very faint, making it hard to distinguish one colour from another. In a similar way, chakras can manifest bright or faint colours, enabling me to determine the health of a person's energy.

Once this was established, I realised that it was possible to adjust any chakra that seemed to be out of balance. To do this, I either focus my attention directly onto the specific chakra, or circle my finger above it in the direction that I want it to go. This quickly brings all the chakra to the same coloured intensity, but more importantly, spinning at the same speed. I have no idea how I am able to do this but people are always aware that adjustments are being made, although they can never quite describe the sensation.

While faintly coloured, slow moving chakras can indicate blocked energy, delicate shades are also visible in elderly people or the sick. As our life force fades, chakras spin much more gently. That's not to say that they are in any way slower, it's just that the motion seems 'lighter', almost like feathers moving in circles. I was particularly aware of this movement within my mother. Mum suffered a stroke nine years ago and I have lost count of the times that the boys and myself have sent healing energy to her. Whether by her side, at work, or at home, we are never too busy to stop whatever we are doing to help her. She is so much better now, lovingly cared for by my father and will soon celebrate her ninety-third birthday! She always enjoys the healing energy we send her, remarking on the beautiful shades of colours she is able to see with her eyes closed, even when we are not with her.

At first I was nervous of sending her energy, in case something went wrong or that it may be too strong for her, but I should have known better and trusted our abilities as she obviously seemed to. In fact she was more worried about us becoming tired doing it, rather than how much better she would feel. One reason I particularly love sending energy to my mother is that, without fail, I always see fairies.

Fairies

I grew up listening to stories about fairies. In fact they have been part of my life for as long as I can remember. Every night as Mum tucked us up in bed, she would tell stories of a family of fairies that lived at the bottom of our garden. These stories could span a few nights, leaving us wondering what the end of the story may be each evening and seemed a great ploy to get us to sleep.

Mother has always loved fairies and recently I asked her where this interest came from. She did not remember, but said how she liked the whole idea of the possibility that these tiny magical creatures, share our world, hidden from the human eye, yet visible in our imagination. She is not alone in this fascination and fairies have a long, somewhat complicated history which goes back to pagan times. Fairies are said to be able to connect the heavens, the earth and the underworld and reside in nature.

The ancient people of Ireland were very spiritual, living in harmony with nature. They respected the natural world all around them, believing that it contained magic, which was especially found in certain trees. Rowan trees were known for their connection with fairies, with their berries being used as protection against evil. The yew, hazel, hawthorn and elder were thought to contain magical properties, and hawthorn are still believed to protect sacred sites from long ago. Because of this, lone hawthorn can still be seen dotted all over Ireland, known as fairy thorns, a meeting place for fairies or *sidhe*. They remain untouched, especially around ringforts and it is believed to be extremely bad luck to disturb them or, worse still, to cut them down. Farmers leave them well alone, affording us a small window into the past, as we admire their twisted and contorted beauty, aged by many more winters and summers than we will ever see.

I first saw fairies, as always, through my third eye, standing in small circles on the floor between my mother and myself whenever I sent her a heartlink. They appeared to be very small, around five or six inches high and seemed to be somehow attached to each other. Unlike angels, fairies did not appear to have large white wings. Their wings are much more colourful, similar to creatures of nature, such as butterflies, moths, and dragonflies. Fairy energy is rarely still and is constantly moving, often in quick darting movements. I often think it rather strange, that angels have such large wings, yet do not appear to use them; while fairies, having much smaller ones, flit all over the place. Another distinct difference between these two energies is that while I never see the feet of angels, fairies' legs and feet are crystal clear.

Fairy energy is very gentle, yet somehow communicates the importance of living life to the full. Fairies have a great sense of humour and I always seem to be aware of giggling whenever they are near. They also have a playfulness that is endearing and often appear to be dancing. I struggled somewhat with the fact that fairies can dance. Surely dancing is a human activity. Angels didn't dance, so why should fairies? Was it just because I could see their feet and therefore movement or was I imagining the whole thing and fairies were just a figment of my imagination? I received an answer to this perplexing question much sooner than I had expected in two separate incidents.

One afternoon I was quietly working with a six-year-old girl when she told me that she could see fairies dancing along the windowsill next to us. This comment came out of the blue, yet I simply smiled over at her while we carried on colouring. My curiosity soon got the best of me, as I was now also watching them through my third eye. I asked if she might like to describe them to me, which she did so in amazingly accurate detail.

Quite soon after I began to give healings again, I was approached by a friend. She was having great difficultly settling her three-year-old daughter at night and the child seemed to be very agitated. No matter what her parents did to see to her needs, she was unhappy. I could see how upset they were about this situation and so I agreed to try to help.

Taking her into a quiet room on our own, I sat her down on my knee. I don't often do healing work with children as I am conscious that they may quickly become restless, making it difficult to concentrate properly. To distract her, I picked up a book and began to read a story, while calling in the angels at the same time. She was soon totally relaxed in my arms, which was amazing in itself as she was usually so difficult to settle. In fact she was so quiet that I stopped reading, unsure of whether she was listening to the story at all.

Looking down I whispered, 'Are you enjoying the story?'

'Yes,' she whispered back, 'but I'm watching the fairies over there on the bookshelf too. Look!' She pointed to a set of shelves in the corner of the room. Glancing over to where she was pointing, I could see nothing.

'Oh,' I replied, slightly thrown off guard, not sure what

to do or say next. We sat together in the silence for a few moments, until finally, curiosity got the better of me.

'What are they doing?' I asked, waiting with bated breath for her answer.

'They are dancing.' she replied.

11

Falling in Love
with Nature

As my world continued to open up to a seemingly endless
variety of energetic vibrations, I was introduced to the
world of animal spirits. Animal spirits, being similar to
those of humans, often linger in this world after their
death. Considering I was supposed to be helping nature,
this vibration took the longest to access, perhaps simply
because of the obvious language barrier. More likely
though, it was due to my continuing reluctance to accept
what was happening to me.

While some people are aware of the angels
surrounding me, others see a variety of animal spirits at
my side. It is said that every person has at least one animal
spirit which stays with them at any given time, yet I am
told that I have many, all the time. These include a wolf,
an owl, bats, mice and a black dog similar to a Labrador,
which sits with its head on my lap. How can I not see
them! Other animals also seen are large multicoloured

butterflies and dragonflies.

I spent many hours wondering why these animals are with me, but could never come up with a good answer. While exploring the world of angels, fairies and spirits had been fascinating, the thought that animals might be protecting me from harm resonated with me. I genuinely wanted to know why so many of them were there. Was my life in danger or did I really have a role to play in saving animals in this lifetime and were these animal spirits there to help me do this? Had I been given this unique opportunity to put my time on earth to good use by bringing the plight of nature to people's attention through a book? Was this a chance to help everyone move forward with a clear conscience, as we attempt to leave a smaller carbon footprint behind us? This was something our ancestors wouldn't have even considered as they followed centuries of beliefs and traditions, ensuring they lived in total harmony with their natural surroundings.

I have always loved animals and nature, wishing them no harm but maybe this platonic relationship wasn't enough anymore. I was doing nothing in particular to protect either the planet or wildlife. But what could I do?

If only they could talk

If animals could speak, what would they say to us? Now that I was acutely aware of orbs, auras and chakras, I began to seriously wonder. While many of us live in a controlled world reliant on outside stimuli, animals exist in one centred on instinct, something many of us have forgotten. Instincts for survival, food, water, warmth, safety, play and reproduction. Instincts that are incredibly strong and rightly so, for they are imperative for a species to continue. If left alone, animals follow these instincts faithfully, relying on the environment and each other to provide them with all their essential needs.

For example when birds migrate for the winter months, travelling many thousands of miles, they don't set off at any random moment. They sense a window of opportunity within nature that gives them the perfect conditions to begin their long perilous journey, the right temperature, wind speed and length of day, often flying in organised formations to conserve energy. Take the behaviour of an animal when a natural disaster such as a tsunami is imminent. They move to higher ground long before the floods reach the land, ensuring their safety.

Since it is therefore blatantly obvious that animals are highly sentient beings, one would have to seriously question the conditions in which many of them are now forced to live. What are their instincts telling them when they are kept in captivity for our amusement, or bred to only be released to end up as a trophy from a hunting trip? Would they condone being mass bred for human consumption or used as 'guinea pigs' to test the safety of cosmetics? This seems highly unlikely. Would they agree to being forced from their homes, destroyed for logging, palm oil production, agriculture or housing? Would they live in confined conditions all day without stimuli or purpose, as many are, to be a so-called 'pet'?

Do we seriously need to question our thinking behind the whole issue of animal welfare? Have we somehow convinced ourselves that animals do not really understand what is happening to them, pushing any disturbing thoughts about their wellbeing to the back of our minds, hoping that somehow everything is OK? In the previous ten years my eyes had been opened in so many ways and it now seemed right to take a proper look at what was happening in the world around me, in an attempt to understand what effect we were really having on animals.

It seemed a daunting task. One look at a map of the world was nearly enough to put me off before I even started. Living in rural Ireland, many of these issues seemed to be a million miles away from home, while others were surprisingly much closer. I knew the skies were polluted, the oceans and rivers were poisoned, the seas were over-fished and littered with debris. I knew that animals were becoming extinct at an alarming rate and that the human population was growing each year, putting further strain on natural resources, and that climate was changing. My understanding of environmental issues was limited to what I observed around me, had read about or watched on TV, but something told me that I didn't have the full picture.

I decided to take a look online. I had no idea what to expect being quite naïve to social media, but was soon awoken with a sickening jolt. It didn't take long before images of mutilated animals started to stare back at me from the laptop. Horrified beyond words I read of stories that in many ways I wish I had never seen. Poaching of elephants, rhinos and tigers, for tusks, skins or simply pleasure. Whales lured into bays to be killed by local men, for the sake of tradition. Bears forced to dance to entertain holidaymakers, polar bears made to sing through metal plates attached to their jaws, elephants taken from the wild as young calves barely old enough to live without their mother only to spend lives of misery in slavery. Used in the circus and zoos or for elephant rides and selfies, brutally forced to submit to an alien world they do not understand or want to be part of. The hunting of wolves, foxes, badgers, deer, hares, rabbits, and many other species simply for pleasure or under a guise of culling.

I read about the ongoing debate on the use of pesticides that are killing the bee population at an alarming rate, along with many other insects and birds. An intensive farming industry where so many thousands of animals exist simply to be slaughtered for human consumption. Living in cramped conditions, never feeling the warmth of the sun, or any creature comforts, even from each other, but only kept confined in unnatural conditions their entire life. Worse still, new born calves taken from their mothers moments after birth, so that the milk can be used for human consumption.

Then there are the tropical rainforests. An estimated five million species of animals and plants exist there, a conservative figure that may apply to insects alone. About half of these species are localized in their distribution, dependant on various geographical factors or reliant on specific plants or trees. Keeping this in mind, because of the present rate of destruction of these forests, some 17,500 species are being lost annually, through loss of habitat, hunting or deliberate killing. This is a rate of between 1,000 to 10,000 times greater than extinction rates prior to human intervention.

Reeling from so much information, I felt as though I had been tossed into the middle of an environmental nightmare that I very much wanted to find my way back out of, yet knew I never could.

What have we done? For four billion years, life on Earth had been governed by natural selection, yet in the last fifty we seem to have changed everything completely. When did we give ourselves permission to do this? It was a thousand times worse than I could ever have imagined.

After a few sleepless nights with the images of all of these animals running through my mind like an endless freight train, I decided I had to put an action plan in place to help in any way possible and the fact I lived so far away from many of these issues no longer mattered. All these animals were now permanently in my thoughts and nothing could be closer than that.

I began signing petitions and sending donations across the world, helping to finance daring and dangerous rescues of bears and elephants from terrible conditions. Joining thousands of other people, we helped transfer these animals to places of safety where they could live the rest of their lives in peace. We then helped finance a new bus to transport these animals in more comfort as they were relocated many miles away; then pledged more money to help educate the locals on how to earn an alternative income.

I signed up to numerous organisational movements, petitioning governments around the world for change, especially in environmental issues. The protection of orangutans, shot on sight as we delve deeper into the rainforests, stripping it bare of its natural resources and anything else that gets in our way. Ensuring donkeys and horses had adequate drinking water and rest in hot counties where they provide rides to tourists. I paid for a billboard to be erected on a route where dogs were smuggled across a border, ending their lives in a summer solstice ritual when they were beaten to death.

There didn't seem to be a week that I didn't either send money or sign a petition and there was so much to learn. It was almost like being a child again, feeling my way round inside a new world. It wasn't as if there was a river of money to supply this new purpose to my life either, but there was always something to donate to whatever rescue was imminent. To be a part of a global community who shared a common empathy for wildlife and nature was amazing and very rewarding. We lived thousands of miles apart, yet shared the same rush of relief as each animal was saved from wretched conditions. Watching online as an elephant took its first bath in a stream after sixty years of neglect or a blind elephant being led by other rescued elephants to water never failed to melt my heart. Had I really helped make this happen? How I longed to gently touch these animals and communicate how deeply I cared for them. But this was not possible and there were still so many more to rescue.

A new beginning

By 2011 I had begun to make huge changes to my own life. My first decision was to stop eating meat and fish. Now that saving animals had become part of my daily life, it seemed ludicrous to be eating them. I made a promise to myself and every living sentient being, that never again would the pleasure of eating be put above the physical, mental and emotional needs of an animal. This was not to say that I thought all animals were treated badly. I knew of many farmers, some of whom were friends, who took excellent care of their animals. But I did have a problem with factory farming, animals shipped thousands of miles across the world on boats in unnatural conditions and abattoirs. Since it is practically impossible to know where all meat, poultry or fish came from, or how traumatically its life had ended, I simply found it easier to stop eating it. No animal had never done anything to hurt me and I no longer wanted to harm them either. It was as simple as that.

I didn't stop there. Next all dairy products were eliminated from my diet. This now began to involve many more changes to my diet as so much food contains either milk or animal products. Rather than letting it become complicated which it easily could have, I decided to follow a very simple rule. If something grew from the ground then I could eat it and if it was organic, all the better. This simplified everything hugely, especially my weekly shop. It was amazing how many aisles in the supermarkets I no longer went down and how many new ones were found.

It didn't take too long for processed food to catch my attention. Many contain so many additives that one would be forgiven for forgetting what they were buying in the first place. There was nothing else for it, these too had to go and all my meals were started from scratch. Did this become time-consuming? Well that would depend on how you consider time well spent. I am as hungry as the next person after a day's work and the prospect of spending an inordinate amount of time concocting some exotic dish every night just wasn't on my agenda. It didn't take long before I was putting together a healthy stir fry or pasta dish in no time at all.

One might think that my meals were now bland and boring, but nothing could be further from the truth. My plate of food is so colourful that I often have to stop to admire it before tucking in and every meal is delicious.

So many changes! When I began, I had expected to be only helping animals, but inadvertently, I was now looking after my own health. How could it be any other way when I had eliminated so many toxins from my diet. I slept well, looked good and felt so much happier.

Next, I decided to address my cosmetics and toiletries. There seemed little point in trying to look nice, if an animal was paying a painful price for it. It was so hypocritical. It didn't take long to find alternatives in my local health shop, alongside many household products and toiletries, which I hadn't expected at all. These too were 'animal friendly' and more often than not, 'organic'. I had no idea these things even existed before. It became quite a challenge to change every item of both my make-up bag and household products to non-toxic options, but I persevered, changing one item at a time. When I ran out of something, I simply replaced it with the organic alternative. Again, while endeavouring to eliminate more cruelty to animals from my life, I found an additional benefit for myself. When reading the labels of various products, I was shocked by how many toxins we were applying to our bodies in the name of beauty.

I no longer wanted cut flowers as presents and since chocolates and cosmetics were also a no-no, everyone was running out of ideas of what to get on my birthday or for Mother's Day. In desperation they decided to buy plants for the garden instead. This turned out to be a good idea, as when it began to fill up with new young shrubs and bushes my attention turned to the garden and I started to notice the nature around me.

Dandelions, foxglove and buttercups, which had once been considered a nuisance, were no longer dug up as 'weeds' but left to live side by side with these new plants and countless people admired the combination. My container of slug pellets was tossed into the bin after reading an alarming article explaining how they were the cause of wiping out the song thrush and hedgehog as both of these animals eat slugs. Horrified that I may have been inadvertently poisoning them, the slugs were left alone to eat any plants they pleased. Once those plants were gone they were never replaced and funnily enough none of us missed them either. As this style of gardening took over, many more birds, butterflies, bees and other insects began to visit our garden, settling on an expanding variety of wild flowers to collect nectar, uninterested in the cultivated plants I had purchased from the garden centre. Encouraged by this, I decided to do more.

I could no longer bear to look at our two goldfish swimming around in their goldfish bowl inside the house as they had done for the previous ten years. I asked my sons if they would dig up part of the garden for a small pond so we could put them outside. Amidst much grumbling this task was accomplished, but the end result was amazing. Within five years our two fish had multiplied to seventy! Dragonflies and damselflies began to visit the pond to drink as well as many species of birds. Who could have believed so few changes could do so much?

Next, I started buying nuts and seeds for the garden birds over the winter months and the volume of traffic to the feeding stations soared. I didn't recognise half of the birds that came and consulted my battered old bird book endlessly. Still not placated I invested in numerous bird boxes to house our new feathered friends. It seemed pointless attracting them to the garden if they had nowhere to live. Carefully researching where each type of bird liked to nest, my sons were soon hammering in place an interesting variety of structures around our house and garden. And without hesitation birds moved into them, even the two bat boxes which I had been told would stand empty for at least ten years before a bat would nest in them.

Many more visitors to our home began to comment on the changes to the garden, the pond and the wildlife all around us. Stopping to listen to the birds singing in the bushes, comparing it all to a paradise. Realising that I couldn't possibly help nature alone and seeing their genuine interest, I began to explain what I had done and how they too could help. To get them started every autumn I collected seeds from dying flower heads, offering them to anyone who may be interested, to scatter in their own gardens and many left clutching envelopes of seeds like long lost treasure.

The energy of trees

While enjoying all aspects of nature by this stage, I was particularly drawn to trees. Their timeless magnificence fascinated me. I would spend every spare moment I could admiring them, enjoying their sense of deep mystery and solitude. They had watched over the lands for many years, seen so many changes, endured harsh winters and the heat of past summers, growing ever taller, wider and always more beautiful. I was already aware of the unspoken communication between all living things, as it vibrated around me, but I was especially aware of it in regard to trees. I couldn't always sense it, but can clearly remember a time when it was remarkable.

I had been feeling particularly downhearted at the time, although I don't remember why. While walking the dogs through the fields, I decided to send a heartlink, asking the angels for some support. As energy began being channelled back to me, I realised that it wasn't coming through me as usual, but from around me. Fascinated I stopped walking to work out where it was coming from, distracted from my initial request for help. I could clearly feel energy being channelled to me, yet not from an angelic realm. Standing in the silence a moment longer, I suddenly realised that it was coming from the trees, but not all of them, only specific ones. An old sycamore in front of me, a large ash to the side and a hawthorn behind. I was stunned. Astonished that, not only could this happen, but that I could feel it too.

How was this possible? I knew angels and spirits were able to read my thoughts, but surely it was beyond reason that nature could do this too? Was it possible that there was one collective consciousness through which everything could communicate? It was obviously time to learn a bit more about trees.

Trees play a vital role in the natural world. They support millions of life forms such as small mammals, birds, insects and plants and provide us with clean air and shade. As natural air filters, they filter pollutants like oil, gas and petrol around us and absorb carbon dioxide from the atmosphere emitted from power stations and many other manufacturing processes. If that isn't amazing enough, they then use the sun to combine the carbon dioxide with water, which they have absorbed from their roots in a process called photosynthesis to grow. We all know that without oxygen we cannot live, so trees should really be regarded as our best friends. After all I have discovered about the animal world and how we are affecting every species by the way we live today, I had hoped for a happier read on trees. I was disappointed. Worse, shocked. As I studied this subject further it appeared that yet again we have pushed the natural world to its limit.

Ever since our ancestors began felling trees it seems to have almost become an obsession. Trees have been used throughout the centuries, to build ships, weapons and homes. They have been cleared to grow crops or for grazing, used as fencing to mark out boundaries and as firewood to cook food and heat our homes. In Ireland alone, this practice has brought the number of trees to the lowest in Europe, with a tree cover of only two per cent in the whole country. What is left is minimal. None of our native woods remain intact. This is so disappointing as trees have been associated with Irish culture for centuries.

The Irish people revered them. So much so that in the fourth century the Irish language was translated into the written word using an alphabet called Ogham, which was based on the names of trees. As I gaze at what remains of trees in Ireland, I can't help but wonder how different the countryside must have once looked. Whereas now we look out over an endless ocean of flat green fields set to grass and crops, it must have once been hundreds of miles of uninterrupted tree cover, providing homes and sanctuary for billions of plants, insects and animals. An oak tree alone can support 450 species, closely followed by willow and birch, which support over 300 species each. Can you imagine the air quality of long ago or the quantity of wild animals and plants that lived in these times? The birdsong alone must have been staggering. How could I possibly help with a mammoth man-made problem, this time, right on my doorstep and why couldn't we just leave nature alone? There seemed only one thing for it. I was going to have to plant trees. Lots of trees.

12

Devarlah

One of the advantages of living in the beautiful Irish countryside is that most, if not all houses are situated on a small piece of land and by some stroke of good fortune, ours came with just under three acres. Up until this point we had split the land between a garden, an orchard, a rather erratically managed vegetable patch and a field for our old horse, Lassy.

Lassy was no ordinary horse and came to us quite by chance. She was a beautiful chestnut sixteen hands mare, previously owned by a local farmer. He had successfully bred many fine foals from her and when we first met her she had been retired to a small field next to ours. It didn't take long before we began to feel sorry for Lassy's lonely existence. With little room to roam, she was often found standing staring silently out of the gate and I wondered what she was thinking and longed to comfort her. We grew increasingly worried about her. Thomas seemed particularly aware of her plight and every afternoon straight after school he would go down to her, taking some fresh water and apples.

On one of these visits he happened to speak to the farmer. He told Thomas that he would be selling Lassy that week at a horse fair being held in the next village as he no longer had any need of her. Horrified, Thomas ran home with this news and I went straight back down to ask if this was true and to whom would he be selling her. He said she would probably be sold for slaughter as she was too old to be of any use to anyone now.

Shocked that her life would end in such a way, I offered to buy her. Taken aback by this gesture, he insisted that I pay the same amount as he would have got for her at the fair. Therefore the next day I handed over four hundred pounds, an amount I could ill afford. The reins of Lassy were put into my hands, with a warning about not bringing her back if we had any difficulties looking after her. Struggling to keep my temper, Lassy and I turned as one from the farmer and together walked side by side along the quiet country road until we reached home. The last five years of Lassy's life were transformed with genuine love, proper care and attention. They were also sometimes spent in the company of other horses when we found other horse owners willing to share their fields with us. This time it was our turn to stand at a gate as we watched her gallop across the meadows with her new friends or lazing contentedly on the grass in the warm sunshine. I never grew tired of admiring her beauty nor the sense of wonder that not only had we saved her life, but had also filled it with so much pleasure.

But when Lassy died of old age our field fell silent once more. I missed her terribly. The tack hung on the old stable door, a constant reminder of her happy days with us and there never seemed to be quite the right reason to take it down. The boys had now left home too and I seemed adrift with endless spare time and memories that I longed to relive.

So it seemed the perfect time to consider transforming Lassy's field into a small wood, filling this gaping void in my life. Planting large numbers of trees and woodland flowers was nothing like any of the gardening projects I had ever undertaken before, in fact it was on a monumental scale compared to any of my previous attempts. It was also a subject I knew precious little about, although I seemed to be learning new facts about nature daily at this stage. I thought it a good time to begin some in-depth study of how to go about planting a replica of the once resplendent woodlands of Ireland.

I was soon engrossed in all kinds of interesting facts and figures about trees. Fascinated to discover that if they hadn't self-seeded naturally, then they liked to be set in groups of threes or fives with the same species. I learned that certain kinds thrived better next to particular trees and that none liked to be set alone. Could this be true? I had often seen trees standing alone in the middle of a field or garden and had always thought that they looked rather striking, never pausing for a moment to consider whether they were happy with this state of affairs or not. The thought that trees had preferences was a revelation. Did they really need similar trees around them to thrive, almost like family and friends?

I recalled how their energy had felt when they had reached out to comfort me. Could they also do this to other trees of the same species? Were trees much more similar to every other living thing than I could have ever imagined? For some reason I had always assumed they were different because they were stationary. How naïve this seemed now. I was going to have to expand my way of thinking more than ever, realising that planting a wood was going to be absolutely nothing to do with what I would want and everything to do with what the trees needed.

The more I read, the more it all began to sound rather complicated. The perfect soil, drainage, exposure to wind and sunlight. Correct staking and weed control. One book suggested that the best place to start an endeavour such as this was to go outside and explore the trees of the locality as they were obviously well-suited to the area. This seemed perfectly sound advice and so the next morning I set off across the fields to study some trees.

The first thing that struck me was a serious lack of mature trees to study at all. In fact it soon became obvious that a tree's very survival seemed to have nothing to do with ideal conditions and everything to do with whether a landowner tolerated them on their land or not. This was blatantly obvious either by their complete absence or by being confined to ditches. This seemed terribly sad. At one time they were so revered by the people that if one was cut down, the punishment was to have livestock taken from the person who did it, the amount of stock taken determined by the species of tree. How could it have come to an almost blatant disregard for the welfare of trees. Even where I found some that had survived, many were cut back severely on both sides so that they wouldn't scrape passing machinery or cars. It felt as if their very existence was a nuisance.

Disheartened with my findings, I began walking home. Hawthorn, sycamore and ash swayed sadly beside me, appearing to share my glum mood. Surely there had to be something more than this in an area that had once been over a thousand acres of natural bog land?

I decided to turn my attention to the woodland where I sit beneath Autumn, even though this is not a natural wood. Rather than going down my usual path though, I stayed near the edges and it was here that a glimpse of the past could be found. Small oak trees struggled to find some natural light beneath the tall conifers. Hazel, elder, alder, willow, birch, holly and dog rose; guelder rose, wood anemones, mushrooms and many varieties of beautiful ferns scrambling through the undergrowth; all attempting to survive in their natural environment. They weren't the only things struggling to survive either. In shallow pools of water, formed from the ruts left from heavy forestry machinery, I found tadpoles, struggling to stay under an unpredictable water level. Staring down at them and then back to the many plant species, I couldn't help but wonder what was to become of them all in their fight for survival. What would happen when the machines moved in to cut the trees down? Would all these plants and animals be crushed underfoot, and be of no consequence? I was already dreading this day because I would lose Autumn and now there seemed to be so much more to worry about.

My initial mission of tree counting forgotten, I hurried home to find a suitable container in which to put the gasping tadpoles. Trudging home a short time later, a bucket of slopping muddy water splashing all over my feet, the tadpoles were relocated to the garden pond. A few months later, I was delighted to see tiny frogs and toads hopping around between the stones. I had never even seen a toad before. I was so pleased to have been able to help them, that there was only one thing for it, my project would now have to include a pond large enough to relocate as many frogs and toads as possible before the trees were cut down.

Work began and by a stroke of good luck, Thomas decided to return home at the end of his final year in university while he waited for a job offer. Thrilled to have him home, I told him of my plans. His response wasn't quite so enthusiastic when he heard of the scale of this latest endeavour, nor the fact that it would more than likely involve vast amounts of his time. Warning that he may not be there to see the whole project through to the end if a job came up, we sat down and began some serious planning. Where to position the trees? Where to lay paths and benches? Waiting for heavy rainfall to study the natural soakage of the land so we could position the pond. Pacing the field again and again to establish the accurate quantity of trees to buy and then marking and strimming each plot.

Armed with the list of trees we needed, we visited local nurseries to establish where we could find not only the best quality of tree, but also the best prices. It seemed that bareroot trees were the cheapest, but much slower to grow and they also needed to be planted straight away. But the price of a few hundred potted trees made my head spin, so we were left with no other option. But how does one go about planting two-hundred trees at the same time! More planning was needed and a lot of extra help. Inviting anyone we could think of who was reasonably fit and healthy, a day was set for planting.

As the sun rose on the morning of April 24th 2012, so too did the people who had offered their help. First to arrive was Lee with a small band of men, closely followed by various friends, relatives and neighbours and in perfect weather conditions, seemingly sent straight from a heaven watching over us, everyone set to work. Thomas became site manager for the day, ensuring the trees were set in the correct groupings, just as I had read many months ago.

It was one of those days that became etched in my memory forever. Trestles and benches were set out in the field filled with refreshments and fistfuls of wild flowers, crammed into small vases as decoration. While under an ocean of blue sky, amidst much fun and laughter, the young saplings were set and watered.

As the evening sun cast long lingering hues of orange and red across the sky, I stood beside my sons, waving goodbye to the last of our tired and aching friends. Turning to me, Lee flashed me one of his bright smiles.

'Well then Mum. It's done! So what are you going call this wood of yours?'

Smiling back, I didn't hesitate for a moment. The name had been channelled to me many months before, while sitting beneath Autumn one summer's morning, reading a book on woodland flowers.

'It's called Devarlah.'

I hadn't doubted the validity of the name for a moment when I had received it, any more than I had with my own channelled name Thor Shahina; and once again I had gone in search of its meaning, soon finding myself browsing through Biblical Hebrew.

The word 'davar' is a root word meaning 'speak', with the ancient Hebrew understanding of 'speaking' being an ordered arrangement of words. Fascinated that I had found the word at all, further research suggested that 'davar' might actually be better translated as 'order' as in, order from chaos.

In regard to nature, ancient Hebrews believed that wilderness is ordered and cities are chaotic. And that within this wilderness we can slow down and be in harmony just as the animals and plants live in harmony with each other. The phrase 'Ten Commandments' was also mentioned, although I couldn't find it by this term within the Hebrew Bible. Instead it is referred to as 'aseret hadevariym' which literally translates as 'ten orders'. Understood as an ordered arrangement of ideas from God, which if followed, would also bring about peace and harmony.

It was a perfect name for the wood, especially as the years began to pass and I could walk through grasses as tall as four or five feet between the trees. In many people's eyes it may indeed look chaotic, yet to the many varieties of wildlife that now knew it as home, it was anything but. Living in harmony with each other, supporting each other in an endless food chain, were foxes, hedgehogs, rabbits, birds, bats, bees, butterflies and moths, slugs, snails, beetles, ladybirds and hundreds of other insects – it was almost like a world set apart on its own and one that I felt privileged to be a part of.

Every spare moment was spent in Devarlah. Endlessly fascinated by the transformation of a simple meadow into a young wood, I never tired of being there. It seemed almost impossible to believe what had been achieved, and how much I had changed since receiving the gift voucher. If anyone had told me then, that one day I would be wandering barefoot through my own wood, listening to birds singing from the trees and watching butterflies dancing amongst the flowers, with an ability to communicate with angels, spirits, animals and trees, there is no knowing as to how I might have replied. Quite possibly it could have crossed my mind that I was chatting to someone to be avoided at all costs in the future. How my life had changed!

Although in many ways I was still the same person, enjoying the company of my family, friends and work colleagues, there was another side of me that few people knew which needed no other company than my own and nature around me. It was as if then, I could drop the pretence of being like everyone else and be who I was truly meant to be and it was within these moments that I felt truly happy.

As this ever-deepening connection between nature and myself grew, I felt a strong urge to do more. Other than giving up my job, which I couldn't afford to, there didn't seem to be much else that could be done. Every evening after work, my time was taken up supporting a variety of wildlife rescues around the world or tending to Devarlah. And what about the book that I was supposed to be writing, which I kept pushing to the back of my mind? Rather guiltily I wondered what the angels must think of me now. Would they be pleased with all I had tried to achieve or was I a huge disappointment? Finding the latter a far more likely scenario, since I hadn't written a single word for them, they probably wished they had picked someone else to communicate with.

How I longed for more concrete guidance from them. Whatever the future now held, there seemed to be no going back. Our lives had changed entirely since angels had entered them. I knew many people were much more aware of the welfare of animals and nature, or had become vegetarian or vegan. Yet how had I managed to change people in this way? Were my words so convincing? Who had I become? Tossing and turning in bed or staring up at the stars in the night sky, I pondered endlessly on what it all could mean.

In desperation I turned to my father, explaining my inner turmoil. I knew I had his love and support in all that I was doing, even though he too had to finally acknowledge that although he knew that I did have some kind of rare gift, he couldn't understand it, as it seemed too impossible to believe.

He suggested that I turn my attention to heartlinking and healing animals, rather than people, something I hadn't considered up to this point. Since I could communicate with spirits and angels, surely communicating with animals should be just as simple and may give me some answers. This seemed a better plan than none and so the word was sent out for sick and injured pets to be brought to the house.

People soon began arriving at the door with an interesting variety of pets. No fancy equipment was in place for their arrival, I hadn't thought that far ahead, but it was free of charge so I worked on the old slate floor. Beginning by laying my hands on the animals, angelic energy was channelled to them. Without fail, the animals began to relax, lying down across the floor, even in such an unfamiliar setting. They then appeared to 'let go' as their breathing slowed, a response I am familiar with myself when receiving angelic energy.

Around me I could hear people exclaiming on how their pets were responding, but I was far more interested in the animal before me. Through my third eye I could clearly see their chakra energy, containing blocked energy leading to illness or distress. Continuing to channel energy, I began by stroking them gently, releasing negative emotions and issues as they sank deeper into the healing energy. No words were needed, communicating only through mutual trust. Each healing took only a few minutes, but the results could be dramatic. Word soon spread and more animals began to arrive.

Then one day Daisy May came into my life and at last I, too, found some peace and answers to many of my questions. Daisy May was a thoroughbred horse housed at a nearby stables, to be trained for professional racing, but who was apparently being uncooperative. Having heard about me, they asked if I could help, as they were becoming desperate in their attempts to settle her.

Horse racing is a sport that I am not at all fond of. I do not agree with these majestic animals been pushed to their limits for entertainment and while it is said the horses enjoy it, I have my doubts. Therefore with many misgivings, I went to visit her. Did I really want to help a horse who would be trained intensively? Would her life be in any way happy?

Taken to her stable, we found her standing with her back to us and the trainer asked if he could stay to watch. Not quite sure what he expected to see, I remembered that I had decided to bring some crystals along to stroke across her back, so at least he would have something to watch. Placing them in the palm of my hand, I held them out to her. In spite of herself she became intrigued and, slowly turning around, came over to me. Sensing her nervousness, I lay them on the floor outside the stable, rather than attempting to touch her and stepped back. Whilst she remained at the stable door watching me, I began to channel angelic energy to her. As the waves of energy reached her, her eyes widened slightly, surprised by the strange sensation. Then her eyelids began to grow heavy, until it was obvious that it was becoming an effort for her to keep them open at all. Eventually she gave up on the battle, letting her head hang down before me as the energy washed over her. Hearing an exclamation beside me, I turned, having totally forgotten about the trainer beside me. He was staring at Daisy May in astonishment.

'Is everything alright?' I asked, slightly worried.

'Yes,' he said. 'But do you know how rare it is for a horse to close its eyes and relax like that?'

'Er, no, I don't,' I had to admit, watching as he started frantically searching through his pockets. What was he doing?

'I have to get a picture of this,' he said and was soon busy trying to get the best shot of Daisy May, who was now lost in some other world than our own.

And it was in this rather unusual setting, that I suddenly understood what I was able to do so effortlessly and how difficult I had been making everything for myself. People never seem able to describe the effect a healing has on them, but watching Daisy May I could see it for myself. And while everyone responded to channelling in exactly the same way no matter what their problems or illnesses may be, I could feel her total acceptance of it, as she placed her trust me, fully becoming a part of the healing process.

As angelic energy penetrated each blocked chakra, toxic emotions and traumas which were affecting her ability to be at peace were triggered. I watched the stories from her past unfolding through my third eye, as each situation was brought to the surface so that they could be safely released. The heartbreaking separation from her mother as she was led away. Confusion. A fear of men because of this and a fear of facing the unknown, alone. My heart went out to her and, staying within the energy of the heartlink, I stayed with her, willing her to let go of these traumatic memories forever so that she could move forward into a new healed lifetime. When the healing energy gradually faded away, she lifted her head and as we gazed at each other, I knew that we had both been part of a rebirth. Both hers and mine.

13

Heart and Soul

Having realised what needed to be done, namely, concentrating most of my time on helping nature and animals, every effort was made to set aside time each day for this endeavour. Each morning and every night, a heartlink was sent to Mother Earth and the whole of the animal kingdom. There was no point in trying to focus on any one particular issue as there were so many thousands to consider.

It didn't take long to realise that these heartlinks were very different from those I sent to people. The main difference being that the transfer of energy was simply enormous. In fact, it was so strong that it could temporarily unground me, making me feel slightly off balance as it swept through my body. Calling on all angels who needed to use me as a link to nature, it seemed as if my whole being opened up to allow the transfer of angelic energy that flooded through me.

Whereas when heartlinking people there would be a direct connection between their heart and mine, this too felt very different. It seemed as though I became the flood gates of a huge river, which when opened, allowed water to flood everything in its path. It was no ordinary river either, but one that encompassed hundreds of thousands of miles. Travelling through air, beneath seas, over mountains, across rivers and lakes, making its way to wherever it was needed. Incredibly, through my third eye I was able to watch some of the animals that the energy was reaching. Eagles soaring high above cliff-top nests, elephants moving slowly through dense jungle, tigers, panthers and many other species. But most disturbingly, images of animals that were suffering, urgently in need of some love and care. Dancing bears tied to posts with no creature comforts or water, caged wildlife and orphaned elephant cubs. I could feel their pain, both emotional and physical, and my heart went out to them. I wanted to wrap my arms around them all and make everything alright, more aware than ever of the injustice done to animals by human selfishness.

Was this what the angels had wanted me to do all along? Was I part of some plan, helping to connect the heavens to the earth so that angels could directly intervene? My eyes widened at the wonder of such a thought and the privilege of being part of such a process.

It seems impossible to believe that anyone could become this involved with nature without becoming increasingly fond of it. This fact was brought home to me one beautiful spring morning, while returning home from a Sunday morning walk with the dogs. Close by, the sound of a bugle could be heard. Listening intently, I realised that a fox hunt was about to start very close to our home. Vans and cars could be seen pulling up along the roadside near the main entrance to the forest from where we had just come.

I am dismayed by the hunting of animals of any description. Worse still, we knew the family of foxes that lived in the forest, often throwing food scraps out for them, especially when the vixen had young cubs to feed. The thought that men were about to comb through the trees with a pack of well-fed howling dogs to chase this beautiful innocent family to their death incensed me beyond words.

Not hesitating for a second I ran back through the trees towards the fox den. The yelling dogs and men were clearly audible as the hunt began. Reaching the den long before they arrived, I turned to face the direction from where they were approaching and began a heartlink, pouring my heart and soul into a call of help from the angels. Within seconds, I felt their response and a strong force of energy passed through me that almost took my breath with it. At the same time I became aware of an extremely heavy weight on my back between my shoulder blades and somehow knew that I had changed form. Although clearly still standing among the trees, my energy had somehow transformed. White light left the centre of my chest in a combination of bright light and speed, sweeping through the trees in every direction. It looked similar to how snow might in a blizzard, shrouding the forest in a heavy mist. Trying to gauge what was happening, the 'snow' settled along the ground and I knew it was covering all traces of a fox, thus preventing any success of finding a scent to lead the dogs to the den.

Amazed by the visualisation and my immediate understanding of it, I was conscious of the vast number of angels who had both heard and answered my call for help. I listened intently for the sound of the hunt, which had gone strangely quiet. My passionate feelings towards the protection of the foxes had intensified my ability to transfer energy to a whole new level. Even though anger had been my initial reaction, the resulting energy contained no malice or negative intention towards anyone or anything.

Also, considering the rather dangerous position I was putting myself in, I felt no fear in facing the hunters. If need be, I would have challenged them in order to protect the foxes. But no hunt arrived and fifteen minutes later the men returned to their vans with their silent dogs and left. Peace was once more restored to the woods and, slightly bewildered by the sudden turn of events, I went home.

Later that evening, watching the vixen playing safely with her cubs in the meadow below the house, I couldn't help but marvel at both their safety and what had taken place.

Life continues...

Travelling to work each day, the nature outside the car window now had my full attention. Whereas before, I would have enjoyed listening to music, I was content to travel in silence, watching the distinct changes visible through the four seasons of the year or the approach of the night sky.

It didn't take long before I began to notice injured wildlife lying along the roadsides. Pulling up next to them, sometimes just to move an animal away from the roaring traffic to somewhere quiet to die, or picking them up and placing them gently in the car. None were left alone. Once sightless to this dilemma, the boot of my car now contained all kinds of paraphernalia for all eventualities. Boxes, gloves, blankets, water and food. Frequently late for work or meetings, I stopped to rescue foxes, badgers, a huge variety of birds, owls, rabbits, hedgehogs and frogs on my travels. No animal was ever too small or insignificant to help and miraculously I still managed to hold on to my job.

These changes didn't mean that I disconnected from people around me. In fact, many more entered my life. Involved with vets, wildlife rescue centres and sanctuaries across the country, we worked tirelessly helping in any way we could, each using our own unique skills. Whatever time of day or night, it never seemed an inappropriate moment to help save wildlife, injured in a human world so different from their own. Overhead power lines, fast-moving traffic, intensive agricultural practices, poisons, pollution, hunting and discarded fishing tackle. Sharing long driving distances, animals were transported across Ireland to relevant sanctuaries. Meeting in various locations, the injured animals were gently passed along a chain of people for the next stage of their journey.

Some of these rescues have included an interesting variety of animals, my favourite being a short-eared owl with a broken wing. A rare visitor to Ireland, it sat staring silently at me for the entire duration of the journey from the passenger seat as we travelled through the night together.

While all of this was happening Devarlah was also maturing beautifully, complete with a pond for frogs and toads. Buzzards, kestrels and sparrowhawks soared high above, hopeful of an unsuspecting meal and even a family of otters travelled across the fields from the river for a frequent look. Life felt good and it seemed as though I was at last achieving something worthwhile. Perhaps angels were smiling down on me at long last. Then one day a phone call upset the whole apple cart.

The city beckons

Can you imagine being offered the job of your dreams? Everything you had ever wished for. One that you knew would give you great job satisfaction in an area of work that interests you enormously. The wages and hours are perfect. Generous holiday and sick pay and health insurance all part and package of the deal and a good pension to see you through your latter years. It is everything you had ever hoped for and worked hard towards. Well this is what was offered to me one morning. Everyone immediately told me to accept it, even my boss! Maybe she was sick of me being late after all, but hadn't known how to say it. But there was one huge problem, the job was based many miles from home in Dublin. There was no question of a commute as the distance was too great, so a move to the city would be inevitable. But that would mean saying goodbye to everything I had come to love, including Autumn and Devarlah.

Autumn has become almost like a shrine at this stage, covered in garlands of flowers that I carried down from the garden, to be woven through her branches. I had long ago realised that Autumn was the tree that the medium Sally had spoken about when I had used my gift voucher. It was exactly how she had described it to me and she had been right, the tree was impossible to describe or distinguish to any specific variety.

How could I leave them behind? Commonsense must prevail in this situation though. Surely financial security far outweighed the importance of such things. It was hardly as if I was going to save the world with my small wood, good deeds and heartlinks. Money could still be sent to various charities across the world and online petitions signed. I could continue to be involved in wildlife rescues, I would just be based at a different location. I could try explaining to any prospective buyers of my house how the wood provided home and protection to countless animals and insects and would they look after it as I had. But what about the bird houses fixed on every wall of the house? Would they leave them up? Would they mind the bats living next to a bedroom window, their only sound being a slight flutter of wings when they returned at dawn. Would they enjoy the jackdaws' friendly squawking from their home in the chimney, or would it be cleared out without a second thought. The beehives, fox den, hedgehog nests, and beds of nettles where the butterflies lay their larva to keep it safe from predators, and my wildflower garden. Would these be destroyed if the new owners decided to tidy the whole place up?

In a panic I rang Ellen to hear her thoughts on the whole matter and we were soon in town chatting over a coffee, discussing it from every angle but no answer could be found.

'Look, why don't we go to Dublin for the weekend, get a feel for the place and see what you think?' she suggested.

'It's a bit short notice for a weekend away don't you think?' I replied doubtfully. It's Wednesday already. How do I make a decision like this over a weekend?'

'Have you a better idea?'

I hadn't and a silence hung between us.

'Well I do know there is a Mind, Body & Spirit Festival on there this weekend if that helps? I was going to ask if you wanted to go to it last week, but forgot about it.'

This made the trip sound much more appealing and

we began making plans.

By the time we reached the capital on the Friday evening, we had already stopped twice on the road to pick up a young hedgehog and a kitten that I had spotted in distress. We then had to drop them off at two separate rescue centres, so by the time we reached the city, our first day had all but gone and we didn't get to see either the city or the Festival that evening.

Things didn't improve much the next day, when we went to St Stephen's Green to eat our lunch. While unwrapping our sandwiches, I spotted a bee on the ground. Bending down, to take a closer look, it was obvious that it was dying. I knew that bees do not simply settle on the ground like this to die, only doing so when they are exhausted from lack of food or water.

'I need a saucer with some warm water and sugar in it,' I said, turning to Ellen.

'What on earth for?' she replied, looking up in astonishment.

'There's a bee that needs some food or it's going to die,' I said pointing at the ground.

Ellen glanced down at the bee and then back to me. 'You're joking, right?'

'Not really, no,' I replied. Silence fell between us.

'Well where are you going to get a saucer and sugar in the middle of a park. Eat your sandwich for heaven's sake,' Ellen snapped. She was obviously getting fed up with my rescues.

'I can't sit eating a sandwich while a bee is dying beside

me,' I said firmly. 'I'll go and find a cafe and see if they will help.'

Ellen looked at me as if I had gone mad.

'You can't do something like that in the middle of a city. Can't you give it some bread instead?'

This time it was my turn to be exasperated. 'Don't be ridiculous. When was the last time you saw a bee eating bread?' Bending down I gently scooped the bee up onto a piece of paper from the sandwich wrapper and put it on the bench next to a horrified Ellen.

'I'll be back in a few minutes. Keep an eye on it while I'm gone.' And with that, I left an open-mouthed Ellen behind.

Twenty minutes later I returned, carefully carrying a cup and saucer containing the remedy and I could see Ellen was not impressed.

'You are crazy, do you know that! People are staring at you.'

'Let them,' I replied. 'They might learn something useful.' And with that I gently tipped some water out of the cup into the saucer and placed the bee on it too. It drank greedily for a full five minutes, until it began to take some interest in its surroundings, occasionally washing the sugar from its feelers. Enchanted I watched, having forgotten where we were, captivated as ever by the beauty of nature. Three curious children from the next bench had joined me at this stage, intrigued by what I was doing. Explaining to them what I had done, I told them how simple it was to help nature.

When the bee flew away and the children were called back to their mother, Ellen turned to me.

'You're hopeless, do you know that? You couldn't go around doing things like that if you lived here. People would think you are completely nuts. And what are you going to do with the cup and saucer?'

'I'm going to take it back of course, what did you think I was going to do with it? Keep it?' I retorted.

'Well I'm not coming with you. What must they be thinking?' Pausing for a moment, she then added, 'What on earth did you say you needed it for? Did you have to pay for it?'

'I told them what I was doing and they were fascinated and really nice about it, so no, I didn't pay for it.'

Getting up from the bench we fell into step walking back through the park. Ellen stayed quiet and I knew she was annoyed with me, mystified by my behaviour. Was I ruining our weekend away? It was our first argument in ten years of friendship and I couldn't help wondering if we were the first people who had ever fallen out over a bee.

When Sunday morning arrived I made a promise to myself not to spoil our last day with any more rescues. Driving around the city we passed the buildings where my job would be based and we tried to get a feel for the place. After a while we had to agree that this was impossible on a Sunday morning when the streets were so quiet.

After some lunch we headed off to the Mind, Body & Spirit Festival and were soon browsing around the interesting variety of stands; animal rescues forgotten. Everything was going well until we decided to go to a talk on angels. Sitting in a semi-circle with a group of about fifteen people, we listened to a talk being given by a man I had never heard of before.

I don't remember what it was about exactly, but do remember the discussion afterwards. Everyone started asking questions about angels that always seemed to relate back to themselves. How could they begin to see them? Was there an angel standing by their side and if so, what were they saying and what did they look like? Then the whole discussion about soulmates opened up. How could they meet their soulmate, fall in love, be happier etc etc. Everyone seemed so caught up in a pursuit of personal happiness, that it felt as though no one really understand the whole concept of angels at all, nor what their messages were really about.

Remembering the message I had received from the angel in London, asking me to remind everyone to learn to love everyone and everything from the heart again, I bit my tongue, deciding not to join in the discussion in case I ruined it. I admired how the man dealt with the questions though, as I'm sure I would have lost my patience, confirming that I would never be good at giving talks or interviews about angels. Then he turned and invited me to join the discussion, asking for my thoughts on the subject of angels. I'm sure he must have been sorry.

'I'm sorry, but I'm not sure if I'm missing the point here. Aren't angels all about love, love of everything and each other?'

Dead silence met my question. I tried again.

'Do you think it's possible that angels are actually guardians of the whole planet rather than just standing beside each one of us trying to make us feel happy? Do they rely on everyone showing unconditional love and respect for every sentient being, ever hopeful that we will do our utmost to protect the planet?' Now I had started, I couldn't seem to stop. 'And that by playing an active part in protecting each other and the planet in this way, we would find the peace of mind that so many people seek?'

This time the silence was deafening. Everyone looked at me as if I had suddenly grown two heads but, more importantly, no one answered the questions and someone guided the conversation back to guardian angels.

As I had thought, no one seemed particularly concerned about the fate of nature, which in a group of individuals who wanted to be connected to angels I found surprising and disappointing.

Fifteen minutes later the talk ended and as we all got up to leave, the man came over to me.

'That was a very interesting slant you took on angels. Do you work with them?' he asked directly.

'No,' I lied, trying not to look at him. I felt like crying. Nothing about the weekend seemed to have gone right. But he persisted.

'Why were you at my talk then?' I looked up at him sharply, was he being sarcastic? His warm smile told me he could see right through my lie and I managed to find an answering smile.

'To be honest I'm in a bit of a dilemma,' I began, while he nodded in agreement. Could he see right through me?

'I'm visiting with my friend for the weekend as I've been offered a job here and I wanted to get a feel of the place.' I then hesitated before continuing.

'Go on,' he prompted.

'Well the problem is this, I'm also supposed to be writing a book about nature,' just about stopping myself from saying for angels. 'And I know that this isn't really the right place to do that. It seems to be taking me years to get around to writing it, but when I do start, I surely need to be surrounded by nature and animals for it to come from the heart. Do you see? How can I possibly write about nature surrounded by buildings, traffic and people?'

Could he see? What on earth was I doing telling a complete stranger my problems.

Smiling at me again, he said, 'Your book will be the first of three. Go back home and begin writing. Good luck with it.' He put his hand out to shake mine.

I stared at him stupidly. 'What do you mean, the first of three?' I managed to splutter out as our hands met.

'You know exactly what I mean,' he said firmly. 'You are not the only one who receives channelled messages from angels.' And with that he turned to speak to someone else.

Ellen appeared at my side.

'What was all that about?' She asked curiously. But

when I turned to look at her, I had no idea where to begin.

'I need to think,' I said after a pause.

Ellen looked at me closely for a few seconds before gathering up our cardigans from the backs of the chairs.

'Come on then' she said. 'Let's go, it's getting late.'

The journey home was in total contrast to the one we had made coming up. I sat staring sightlessly out of the side window into the darkness, lost in thought. Could what he had said be true? If so, that could only mean one thing. There would be no move, no promotion, no new car and no certainty of a secure retirement. Would I risk putting my whole life into the hands of angels, hoping that they would take care of all my material needs instead of securing a good job? It seemed an awful chance to take. The decision that I needed to make made me feel slightly faint.

Seeing the sign for a petrol station ahead, I turned to Ellen. 'Could we stop for a coffee?' I asked. 'I feel a bit sick and dizzy.'

'Of course!' she replied and we were soon swinging the car into the parking area. I couldn't get out fast enough to take in some fresh air, grateful of a gentle breeze pulling at my hair. Ellen stood watching me.

'Are you OK?' she asked looking concerned.

'Yes, I'm fine,' I replied, smiling reassuringly at her. 'I just felt a bit off for a few minutes, that's all.'

We strolled into the shop together and after ordering two coffees sat down at a table, hugging our cups in companionable silence. After a few minutes I decided to tell her all about the conversation I'd had with the man at the talk.

'What do you think?' I asked, when I got to the part at the end when she had come over to me.

'Gosh, that's a spanner in the works isn't it? Three books!' she exclaimed after a thoughtful pause. 'One thing is for sure, there's definitely never a dull moment with you around!'

'Well what do you think I should do?'

'What do you want to do?' Ellen replied firmly.

After a few moments of silence, a wide smile spread across my face and with it, a feeling of excitement began to bubble up inside me, although I had no idea where it came from.

'Do you know what I'm going to do?' I declared decisively. 'I'm going to write that book!' and we both burst out laughing at my authoritative tone of voice, jumping to our feet as one to hug each other tightly, the disastrous weekend already behind us.

As we sat down again to our neglected coffees Ellen suddenly asked, 'What are you going to call it?'

'I don't know, I've never really thought about it – what about *Call of an Angel*?'

Ellen gave this title some serious thought. 'Do you know, I like the sound of that,' she said as we began gathering our belongings together once more to continue on our way. 'It's got a nice ring to it.'

And the story of the gift voucher began.

Appendix I
Thomas's Story

The beginning

The Integrated Energy Therapy ® (I.E.T.®) course was a big step for me. I was somewhat sceptical about the whole situation, but I had faith in my mum and so went along with an open mind.

My life at the time was hardly spiritual and this was not something I would have done of my own volition. Yet my eyes were opened in a way I never thought possible. The course involved inviting angels into your life and awakening to a fascinating reality of healing with angels. letting images come into our minds. I was convinced I wouldn't see anything, but to my surprise I saw a great deal. It started out with colours rolling around before my closed eyes and soon all kinds of images started to appear. At first there were lots of eyes, which did seem a bit odd. Yet these images persisted.

The spiritual instructor for the day, Gretta, told me that it could mean that I was able to see things that others do not. I found out some time afterwards, she was right.

Embracing the idea

This new view on life was very different to the one I was used to, and it took quite a while to come to terms with it properly. The idea of angels being not only real but also being able to see them was a lot to take in. I had doubts about whether or not I was really seeing these things, or if any of it was even real. It was natural for me to be apprehensive as I was unsure of any spiritual existence at all.

The angels gave me a whole new lease on life and it was very reassuring to know that no matter what the situation was, I could always ask for help. All I had to do was send a heartlink. At the start I was often reluctant to do this, but as time went on, I began to see how I really could make a difference.

The angels helped me in all kinds of ways, from cheering me up, to helping me understand a situation I could not get my head around. I realised quite quickly that they would only help if what I wanted was for the greater good.

This seemed a bit 'high and mighty', but when I think about it, it wouldn't make any sense if angelic beings helped to cause harm.

Seeing is believing

I saw and still see a great many things: from beautiful people with glorious wings to majestic animals and beings

194

too complex to describe. The first time I saw angels clearly was some time after the I.E.T.® weekend. I was with my mother and we had just finished heartlinking, as we often did at the time purely to see what would happen. After we had finished I went upstairs and something caught my eye in my mother's room. I saw something very faint in the air.

I went to investigate, but found nothing initially. But, by standing still, I began to notice what can only be described as multicoloured clouds floating around the room. Watching closely, these shapes began to take on a clearer form until suddenly I realised that they looked like people, only smaller, and they had wings! I was totally taken aback but there was no mistaking what I could see and no matter how many times I looked away and looked back, they were still there. I tried to show this amazing discovery to my mother, but although she could sense them, she just could not see them as I could. That was the first time I saw clearly with my own eyes what most people can only dream about.

After this first encounter I saw many things on different occasions, but something I see almost constantly is energy. I could not quite grasp what it was at first and can only really describe it as movement in the air, as though there are lots of tiny particles suspended in the atmosphere. These particles can change. Sometimes there is very little of this energy or very little movement, then at other times it seems as though the air is alive, and all the tiny particles are teeming with energy and cannot keep still. I notice this particularly when heartlinking and often what first appears are shapes within this energy. I have asked other people if they can see it, but they were unable to notice the energy in a room. It is clearest in the dark as then you cannot focus on anything else, so the energy is very easy to observe.

Clearing for the first time

It was not long before a new way of using my developing abilities was presented to me, outside of helping those around me. My mother had often mentioned that she sensed spirits while we heartlinked, but we never made any attempt to acknowledge them beyond asking them to move on. I remember asking Mum why she never talked to these spirits to find out why they were here.

I do recall one occasion when this happened. A friend of ours, who is open like us, asked if we could help her with her house. Her youngest son had not been sleeping well and had been seeing strange 'monsters' around his bed. Mum agreed to go over and see if there was anything she could do. As she hadn't done anything like this before, we went together. We had no idea exactly what we were going to do, but knew that we could at least try to help.

We began by heartlinking, and soon enough things started to happen. We quickly became aware of a spirit in the house, but could not locate it and it was not very willing to come to us. This led me to try to see the spirit to find out exactly where in the house it was hiding.

Having seen angels previously, I was confident that I would be able to see a spirit. It took some time but I finally found it sitting on the bottom bunk where our friend's son slept. It moved on with relative ease, but we soon became aware that there was another spirit in the house. After some time I discovered it hiding behind the television in the living room. This was only the beginning of it, though. He had no intention of moving on. As hard as we tried, he would not leave and was not too happy to have us bothering him.

I suggested to Mum that, instead of just trying to move him on, she should talk to him first. Thankfully this worked and she began to find out why he had lingered. It turned out that his wife had gone out to collect wood one day, but never returned. He didn't know what had happened to her and was unable to rest without knowing where she was. In desperation Mum had the idea of asking his wife to help. To my surprise, not only did this actually work, but I could physically see her standing in the room. Her presence encouraged him to leave, and after a while a quiet peace filled the room. At the time we did not know what exactly we were doing but we now know we were clearing the house of spirits and this was to be the first of many.

I am not alone

Something that I came to realise over time was that we are never really alone. There is always some guiding presence there to keep an eye on us. I first noticed this at a time I least expected. I was in bed and could not get to sleep. Lying in the darkness I started to see colours in my room, which began to look like the hazy outline of people. The prospect of having a group of people watching you as you sleep might seem a bit odd, but I felt very relaxed knowing they were there. It was as though they wanted to let me know they were looking after me.

I discovered later that these beings are my guides, and almost every night I can see them in my room. While I do not know much about them, I know they are there to offer me guidance and support. Their presence is not always apparent. They only seem to interact when I seek out their assistance or need some support. This can range from helping me understand something that has been bothering me to simply filling the room with a calming energy. I have never noticed them anywhere beyond my room, but perhaps this is because they are drawn to where I am at rest and free to let my mind relax. While these guides are not always present, they are not the only beings with me. I also came to understand that my guardian angel is often with me, especially if I am not feeling good or if I am upset.

The first time I saw her, she was very clear and was bathed in a purple glow that seemed to emanate from her being. I had been feeling quite low and needed some sort of support. It was then that I felt the room change, as though it was being filled with calm and quiet. As I sat there feeling sorry for myself I noticed her appear at the foot of my bed and she began to reassure me. Before long I was feeling much better about myself. After meeting with my guardian angel I knew that she would always be there if, and when, I needed her. Apart from having the guides with me, there are always the angels who are only a heartlink away. Often when I have felt confused or unsure and have sought their help, my problems begin to simplify and seem more manageable. It is amazing to think how much help and support is available if you only ask, something that I have become very used to doing over the years.

What happens when I heartlink?

It is difficult to say what exactly a heartlink is, as every single one is unique. What I can tell you though is what I experience each time. The most apparent feeling is one of calm: as the heartlink progresses it is as if a trance-like state sets in, and my mind and body relax. I often do not know how long a heartlink has taken as I become engrossed in the whole experience. But whenever I heartlink I still have a sense of what is happening around me, even though I am not sure how I know this. At times I am sure that I am experiencing what is happening within my mind, and at other times it is as if I am seeing it all behind closed eyelids. This is not always easy to do; a heartlink does require a certain amount concentration, which is why I feel some are more effective than others.

Often I notice some very distinct things while

heartlinking, particularly when I have been involved in removing spirits. A very clear experience is when we have been trying to locate a spirit in a house. This can be difficult sometimes; it can be easy to know if one is present or not, but finding one when it is not interested in coming to you is a bit trickier. A few times on these occasions, while heartlinking, I have felt as though my energy has expanded out beyond my body, weaving around the house in search of the spirit, and as this was happening I could see through my closed eyes the various rooms in the house as my energy passed through, seeking out the spirit.

I clearly remember on one of these occasions that when I had found the spirit my energy wrapped around and restrained it so that it could not evade us anymore. Other similar things have happened, but this was by far the most vivid and it is something I was amazed by. I had not realised until then that a person's energy could be used in such a way, but then again there are a lot of things I realised I could do after becoming aware of the angels.

Not everyone is open

As I am sure you are aware, not everyone is willing to accept the possibility of angels or that it is possible to contact them and seek their help. While there are a growing number who are open to it, there are still a great many who struggle to come to terms with the whole idea. The majority of people in my opinion are in this category, even though many might be delighted to accept the angels into their lives.

Most people these days are overly fixated on their earthly existence and the immediate physical world around them. They have become too focussed on what they can see with their own eyes, and thus it becomes difficult for any sort of spiritual entity to become apparent to them. They are unconsciously closed off from a very important part of life. No matter how one views it, spirituality is a key part of our existence, but its importance has begun to wane in recent times as people drift away from it.

To compound this problem, many view spirituality in a linear fashion, putting too much emphasis on religion as the focus of spirituality. I am not discrediting the benevolent influence religion has had on people's lives, but I am reluctant to accept that religion is the complete extent of spirituality. I see it more as a glimpse into a vast existence which is barely understandable to us.

Through mediums we can understand religion as we are given an insight into a realm that is striving to bring good into our world. This is something which has become more apparent since I became aware of the angels in my life.

Helping the people around me

Even though some people are not open, it does not mean you cannot try to help them. Many people I know would struggle to come to terms with the angels and what I can do. I am always conscious of people I know who might need help and one of the easiest ways I can help them is by sending them a heartlink. These people do not need to know that they are getting one and they do not even need to be nearby. Most would not realise the effect it has on them but I can often see that they become more relaxed and light-hearted. Of course, this does not always work; some people can be closed off, making it difficult to help them, but it is always worth a try.

Sometimes I have been with someone who needed my help, and although I was not able to give them a heartlink at the time, I have begun to help them in another way. I noticed that the energy around me began to drift over to this person and wrap itself around them, just like someone putting a blanket around someone when they are cold and gradually they would begin to feel themselves again. After some time my energy came back to me and I could see that I had made a difference to this person's mood without consciously doing anything.

There are other simpler ways that I try to help those around me. I generally try to stay positive and happy: I feel that the people around you respond to how you project yourself, so if you are in a good mood all the time they will react to this and associate you with feeling happy. Of course, life is rarely as straightforward as this, but if you do not try, you will never know.

What would they say?

Have you ever wanted to tell someone close to you something very important but could not? This gift of mine is something like that. There are people in my life who are very special to me, but no matter how I try to word it in my mind, there is no way I can tell them. It would simply be too much for them to handle, and they would probably think I was joking or had gone mad. Thinking of it from another person's perspective, I suppose it does sound a bit 'out there', but it is still an important part of my life, part of who I am.

About two years ago I began to broach the subject with some close friends while on a camping trip. I admit that we were all a little inebriated and my explanation was not the most coherent. This is probably why I was met with such a sceptical response from most of them. I do remember that one of my friends took me quite seriously and the next morning asked me about it again. As I had been discouraged by my other friends' reactions, I shrugged it off as drunken antics. I still think that this friend remembers that conversation and although he has not mentioned it again, I think he believed me.

Although my abilities have made me into the person I am, I do not want to scare anyone off with something I know they would not easily understand. This has not really affected my relationship with others, as I am the same person with them as I am with people who know about the angels. I am sure that there will be a time when

I am able to discuss the angels and everything I have done with others, but for now I am content with the way things are.

My views on life have changed significantly since the I.E.T.® course. I see more meaning in everything I do and in everything I see around me. Actions we take or do not take can have consequences we do not even realise at the time. If I had known then how much that course would have changed my life I may have been more apprehensive, but I am glad that I did it. The people in my life are more important than they used to be. They have become anchors, keeping me grounded and ensuring that I am never alone. Even though the angels and guides are often with me, I still need people I can interact and experience life with. They may never know what I can do, or how I have helped them in the past, but that is not important. I am just glad they are there.

I live my life as fully as I can and I never let myself get caught up in detrimental emotions. I see no point in being angry or unhappy because it takes away from all the good things in my life. I believe that forgiveness is a very powerful instrument, which can change a bad situation into a good one. It is something I highly recommend. I am content giving help where I can and living my life knowing the angels are there if I need them. Perhaps there is some reason why I am able to do the things I can do, but right now I do not know that reason. Life has its own way of nudging you in the direction you need to go so I will leave such matters to the angels. They have not led me astray so far, and I think they are happy with what I am doing with my life. I do not know where they will take me in my life, but when I get there I am sure I will know what to do.

Appendix II

Lee's Story

Opening the door

My story starts the day Mum came back from a weekend away with a friend. They had been on a course where they had experienced encounters with angels. At the time I wasn't really listening closely, so the details are a tad vague. Nevertheless I am certain that it was my Mum who first introduced me to the whole concept of angels.

'Angels' is a broad term that will be bandied about readily from now on so keep in mind that you only see or experience celestial beings as something you are capable of understanding. In my case, because of my partly Christian upbringing, angels were the most plausible form I could identify with. I should state at this point that I do not 'see' in the same way as many others, such as clairvoyants, but tend to experience intense emotions that have been felt by others – a sensation known as clairsentience.

Mum had been practising angel therapy at home regularly after her return from the weekend and would talk to us about her experiences with heartlinks, among other things. Like most people my age I had been nodding and agreeing to whatever my mum was chatting about, but only half listening. However, it happened that, despite my teenage flippancy, I agreed, along with my brother, to go on a family weekend trip to do an I.E.T.® course.

I am always open to new experiences, but as we headed off the following Friday evening, I suddenly began to wonder what I had signed up for. So I wasn't at all prepared when I went for our first session with the rest of the group. I remember there being about ten people present on that day and we were issued a name tag and a notebook. So far so good.

After the usual pleasant formalities, we participated in a group meditation to get us started and then after a brief reflection moved on to the main focus of the course. In order to progress it was necessary to create an initial link to the angelic realm which the Spiritual Instructor explained. This also included a description of the steps that are required to establish a heartlink.

Armed with the necessary information, we began sending heartlinks as a group, one for each of the 'Healing Angels of the Energy Field'. After each attempt we noted what went through our minds in our workbooks. This was then discussed with the group so we could better understand the different ways each person could experience what was essentially the same task. To be perfectly honest, I didn't expect to see anything because I was still doubtful and fairly uninformed about what I was doing there in the first place. Yet as soon as we started the heartlinking process, images began to flow through my mind.

The one image I clearly remember was that of an extremely intricate fountain of light-green protective energy slowly weaving itself around the world. The detail of what I saw that day is probably why it has remained with me all these years. It was as if I was seeing thousands of individual threads of energy weaving an amazingly intricate web through and around the Earth. I was, and still am, amazed by this experience each time I recount it in my mind.

After that weekend I think I knew deep down that my life would never return back into the norm it once was, but I tried.

Beyond the door

As with any new skill, in order to progress we practised heartlinks at home regularly and our experiences became more vivid. A particular point of note in the evolution of our new abilities was when Mum agreed to 'clear' a house for a friend. Clearing a house is when you remove by spiritual means unwanted energy that may be causing a disruption of some kind. This inaugural case came about because the friend concerned was beginning to worry about her child's sleeping problems and especially the vivid nightmares that accompanied them.

Unaware of what lay ahead, the spiritual trident that was our little family congregated at the affected house. Mum led the way and I, despite once again feeling slightly doubtful, obliged along with my slightly more eager younger brother. Not knowing exactly where to start, we began with what we knew best and started heartlinking together. My memory of what happened following this initial action is vague, but I do remember becoming overwhelmed with what I can only describe as an onslaught of pure emotion. It was akin to the feeling you experience when you miss a step, combined with that strange goose-bump sensation when watching something spectacular. I sensed an underlying vibe that felt malicious in some way. These menacing sensations are all I can recall from this house-clearing but Mum said afterwards that for most of the time I was doubled over and sat on a windowsill, oblivious to what was happening. For me it felt like a very short time, but apparently we were there for quite a while and a plethora of strange things were happening. This was the last time I was taken to a house clearing whether I wanted to go or not. I put this exclusion down to Mum's desire to protect me. It must have been uncomfortable for her to see me experiencing such a disconcerting event.

Since that day I have felt all kinds of emotions as a result of my ability, and for a while it was hard to get used to. This was especially true when I was with my friends, as it was hard to suppress some of the stronger emotions that would surface from time to time. I found it difficult to stop these emerging and to keep my ever-strengthening abilities separate from my social life.

In time though, without consciously knowing it, I started to associate certain friends with the abilities that had surfaced. They were the ones who would comment on the twinkle that had appeared in my eyes, or who randomly decided to start talking to me about weird experiences they had in the past. It felt reassuring to hear that other people had experienced extraordinary things too, and they were a big help to me in my ongoing journey.

The necessity for balance

One of my biggest mistakes throughout this journey was my refusal to accept that my approach to life needed adjusting in order to maintain my physical and spiritual self in balance, and that I needed to keep my energy field clear of unwanted dark energy. The easiest way to achieve this is by grounding oneself, but this was something I did not appreciate until Mum began to ask if she could clear my energy field regularly. She suggested this because we noticed that when I had been out with friends on the weekends, I often came back surrounded by dark energy and seemed to be ungrounded. For a household that contained three highly tuned energy fields, this became something of an issue. And it was around this time also that I had a nasty experience with a malicious spirit that had attached itself to me.

This was by far one of the strangest things that has happened to me so far. To say I was possessed might seem clichéd, but it is still the only way I can describe what I felt. It wasn't that I was walking around the place babbling incantations or scribbling weird markings on the walls, but I was having deeply dark thoughts which put me in a foul mood for a couple of days. Mum, as usual, understood what was wrong with me and that it was much more than normal teenage angst. She asked if I would benefit from a heartlink. Begrudgingly I agreed to not disagree, so she followed the steps that had become almost second nature to her and sent me some much-needed energy. Because of the mindset I was in I thought her concern was unfounded, so when I was told that there was a dark spirit in the house that was using me as a hiding-place, you can imagine how I felt.

As this was early on in my mother's development of her abilities, messages were sometimes vague and hard to determine. On this occasion the solution appeared to have something to do with water, so I was instructed to go for a shower, which failed to rid me of my stowaway but, considering my age at the time, was probably necessary anyway.

The next message Mum received was clearer, and before I knew it I was walking down the field at the back of our house towards the river with a bucket of water on one side and a tightly clenched fist of frustration on the other. My instructions were to find a spot close to or in the river, take off my shoes and socks, and pour the bucket of water onto my feet. I was far from impressed but obliged for the sake of some peace and quiet.

The whole process worked, because on my way back my mood changed significantly for the better. It has always seemed strange to me that by carrying out these instructions my entire frame of mind was changed within a few seconds. One might argue that the actual act of watering my feet was a psychologically viable way of cleansing or changing my mood, but this leaves other questions. I was not willingly agreeing to do this and made no attempt to address the issue directly and yet the results were dramatic and instantaneous.

The light of protection

Before I continue with my story I must state that I am not religious, as I strongly disagree with the actions of the many who would use the weakness and suffering of others to better themselves. Barbaric acts carried out in the name of something holy litter our history and continue to poison our integrity as a race every day. This is not to say that I have a problem with faith.

Faith defines some and destroys others. This double-edged blade is the weapon we use to cling on to hope, to justify acts whether good or bad, to better ourselves, to help others, to answer the questions that we as a race cannot come to a conclusion on, and to battle with the continuing struggle that is life. Faith is not necessarily based on religion; one can also find faith firmly rooted in fact or science and it is its versatility that warms me to its cause.

For all the bad that has happened in the world because of faith, there is also a balancing account for the opposite.

Belief plays a major part in all this, so while I refuse to conform to the norms of the religions that have crossed my path so far, I have come to understand that we are all part of an integrated network of energy that flows through us and everything that surrounds us. This energy vibrates at different intensities to create all the wonder we are privy to at any one time, and I believe that it is this energy that millions simply perceive as God.

What I like about my association with angels is that I never really feel alone. That's not to say I feel as if I am being watched constantly, but when I need a boost all I have to do is connect to this vast expanse of energy. I know that if I need to I can send a heartlink and feel very much at ease. This is where I feel what is called the 'Light of Protection'. Being aware of energy makes you feel more at ease about things you cannot control or see. It is said 'what you don't know can't hurt you', but I believe what you do know can give you peace of mind. I see the angels as a light that always surrounds me and protects me from what I cannot see or control.

Is it all real?

I have asked myself this question countless times since all this began and, to be honest, I am not sure I am ever going to get a definite answer. What proof I might have could just sound like coincidence to someone else. Still, I tried my best to get some physical proof so that I could set my mind at ease. The best opportunity to do this came along when Mum told me she had received a message telling her that I could influence the wind or air. When I look back on it now, it seems a bit farcical, but in my young male mind at the time I felt it was a perfect chance to alleviate my suspicions by using my abilities in the most awesome way possible, directing the elements just like a superhero in a fantasy novel.

I spent quite some time trying different techniques, none of which worked, as was to be expected. This feeble attempt, among other things, led me to become increasingly sceptical of the whole situation. I stopped regular practice, not bothering with heartlinks anymore, and generally shut myself off from angels. It wasn't a case of waking up one morning and deciding not to bother anymore; it was more of a gradually fading process over a month or so.

...and the sickness

For most of my life I had suffered from tonsillitis at least once or twice a year. It usually struck when I was particularly run down, fatigued, or had become a bit cold going between classes at school and my doctor would always put me on antibiotics. Each time he would urge me to get my tonsils out, but I am not the sort of person who likes anything forcibly removed without it being absolutely necessary. This particular time was no different, and I went to the doctor, having already self-diagnosed myself with my ailment. He asked about taking them out again, and once more I refused and asked for some pain relief and antibiotics and was on my way. In such situations I would normally be on the road to recovery quite quickly, but this time my condition deteriorated rapidly. The antibiotics I was put on were about as strong as they get and I was being taken to the local surgery each day to get painkillers injected so that I might get some sleep. After three days stuck in this nightmare of an existence my mum came into the room between one of my trips to the toilet to cough up more stomach bile to ask if I would like to do a meditation followed by a heartlink.

Finding myself in a similar situation to the one that started this story and figuring that it couldn't make it any worse, I once again obliged. The meditation helped to set a nice calm atmosphere, but the heartlink that we did afterwards was simply amazing. I had done heartlinks before and felt relaxed and at peace, but this time the things I saw were truly remarkable.

On this occasion it was Archangel Michael who came to me. His presence was immense and there was bright blue light everywhere. I don't remember feeling any of the pain or sickness, and he took me with him to a special place. When we were there he asked me to rekindle my relationship with the angels as they were saddened by my lack of interest. I agreed to redouble my efforts. Michael then unsheathed his sword and drove it into me. We re-entered my body, and when he left I became aware of the pain once more. Afterwards, I'll admit, I lay there crying.

I wasn't sad, although I don't think it was happiness either. On my next visit to the bathroom to empty my stomach of the bile that had built up since my last visit, I brought up a large black blob. It was the most disgusting blob I had ever seen and, being an ex-smoker, that's pretty nasty. But it was seriously black, which was what shocked me the most.

Since that day I have never had tonsillitis or been overly sick in any way. Apart, that is, from the occasional 'man flu', which is really no more serious than an ordinary cold.

Following that bout of sickness which resolved itself quite quickly after the arrival of 'The Black Blob' my resolve was now cast in iron. I began to incorporate the angels back into my life in a more active way. If someone asked for a heartlink, I would send it and, unlike before, they would comment on how nice or helpful it felt. Of course with increased use, my abilities became more attuned and much more powerful.

Wings

Of all the things that I have learned from being connected with the angels and the associated energy, I like the idea of wings the most. Personally I didn't notice mine or even think about having any until I went to a Mind, Body & Spirit festival in a nearby town. At first I thought going to one of these events would be a fun idea. At least there would be other people to mingle with who also had an awareness of the angels. What I didn't think about was all the energy and emotions such a gathering would attract.

When I first got there it was a bit overwhelming, but it was only a minor hindrance and so, grounding myself, I set off about all the different stalls looking at what was on offer.

For the most part it was just a collection of novelty shops with Tarot card readers and their lengthy queues dotted in and around the venue. As I was strolling through all the stalls a woman stopped me and asked if I would like to avail of her therapy. At first I was not quite sure what she was offering, but I graciously declined as it cost more money than I had on me but partly also because it seemed a bit ridiculous to me. The woman persisted and said that I needed to have it done, and she would do it for me free of charge if I came back in about ten minutes when she had finished up with a customer who was lurking around her stall with some intent.

Never one to turn down a gift, I found myself ten minutes later waiting to have my secret lost chromosome unlocked. At the time I didn't feel like anything was happening so I thought nothing of it. Later on though, when leaving the festival, I felt a sensation as if a great weight of energy was on my upper back which felt like an extension of my body. This was, to say the least, a strange sensation, and the best way I can describe it is that it was like having massive wings on my back. This feeling did not last for too long, but every once in a while I am made aware of it again.

The middle ground

What I have found is that no matter how much you ask for, you never get more than what is needed. Of course, if you have a direct link to all-knowing beings, what is the harm in asking for a lucky Lotto ticket once in a while, one might ask? This idea that money is the route to happiness, which is so deeply ingrained in society, does not transcend to the Angelic Realm, as it is mostly a lie we entertain with a rather serious degree of naïvety. People probably do ask for such things, but I do not think that it is the best way to attain happiness. This is not to say that there are not people who have asked for money and received it; but there are still many opportunities presented to us by coincidence or luck and I often find that it is not until you have stopped asking for something that you receive it, and not always in the form you had hoped for.

The world in its current state is a breeding ground for greed, and I believe that it is the angels' intention to try and correct this. All around us we are surrounded by false temptations and actively encouraged to spend money we don't have in order to fuel an economy that is, at best, in a constant state of fragility. This carefully manufactured state of uncertainty is meticulously managed by the minute percentage of the population who make it their life's mission to stockpile more money than anybody can spend in a thousand lifetimes. They manage to keep the masses quiet by letting the uninformed believe that these mega corporations are necessary to keep this circus, known as the global economy, afloat. This massive misconception of reality is single-handedly destroying our planet.

Who is to blame? We are. Every time you conform to this fictional existence you are contributing to the destruction of our only habitat. How foolish we are to focus on preserving a shrinking horde of endangered species when we ourselves are the root cause.

We may be one of the last on this list of endangered species, but if we allow ourselves to get to that point it will be far, far too late.

From now on

For now I have come to the end of what I feel I have to say. What I have gathered from my experiences so far is that I am probably better off the way I am now – which is happy, settled and confident that I am being watched and minded, and that's all you really need. I have given up the hope of winning the Lotto or finding a suitcase full of money in the street. As it stands, that much money would only be spent on a big TV, a big car, and a big house, all of which I don't need because I have a car, a TV, and a house that suits me just fine.

Maturing

Since the beginning of this story, I have come a long way

personally. These days I am a settled man with a lovely girlfriend and a beautiful son, both of whom I love more than anything else. For the first time I believe that I can look inward and know that I am truly happy with myself. I never thought even as little as a year or so ago that I could be so settled and content. However, throughout my upbringing I have refused to conform to the rules and guidelines that we are all made to follow. It's not that I have a problem with authority but rather I tend to disagree with the general idea of the 'system' as it is currently run.

According to the experts in spiritual energy, I fall into the category commonly known as 'Indigo Child' or 'Intuitive Sensitive'. When I discovered what this meant exactly, I found it quite difficult to deny that the description fitted uncannily well. My girlfriend has no idea of what I do, and sadly at the moment I do not think that she would accept or understand it if I told her. Our son is a sparkling light among many others, and I know already that he is minded every second of the day by the angels. He is special too and will have to do his part when the time comes, but for now I'm happy to just watch him trace the energy around the room with his eyes, which sparkle as all eyes do that have angels behind them.

Acknowledgements

A big thank you to everyone who encouraged and supported me in the writing of this book. Special thanks to all my friends, especially Caroline, Ellen, Annemarie, Gretta, Tracy, Carol and David who were there from the start.

Thank you to Josephine Wall for allowing me to use *Spirit of Flight* for the cover. It was a privilege to travel the south of England to meet you and watch, while you painted one of your creations. Such talent and patience!

Thank you to Stephanie Zia of Blackbird Digital Books for deciding to publish my book. I now know the feeling an author gets when their book is accepted by a publisher. Well worth the wait and hard work. Thanks, also, to Janet for her forensic proofreading.

Thank you to my two sons. Without their continuous support and patience *Call of an Angel* would never have made it past the first page. For the hours we spent together at the kitchen table, three laptops open, while we argued and bantered about how best to describe things we had never felt or seen before.

And to you the reader for picking our story to read. May the angels guide and protect you in everything you do.

Patricia x

www.josephinewall.com

Coming Soon from Patricia O'Toole

A Little Piece of Heaven
a book of channelled messages from the angels

For news of when this title will be available, and all Patricia O'Toole news, join her mailing list (managed securely by MailChimp)
http://eepurl.com/c56Qy1

Photo Credits

The Author as a child c. Patricia O'Toole

Bronze statue of Saint Michael at Castel Sant'Angelo (Rome). Creative Commons, CC by Alf van Beem

More Non-Fiction from Blackbird

I Wish I Could Say I Was Sorry by Susie Kelly

Safari Ants, Baggy Pants & Elephants: A Kenyan Odyssey by Susie Kelly

Love & Justice: A Compelling True Story Of Triumph over Tragedy by Diana Morgan-Hill

Schizophrenia: Who Cares? – A Father's Story by Tim Salmon

Tripping With Jim Morrison & Other Friends by Michael Lawrence

Cats Through History by Christina Hamilton

A London Steal – The Fabulous On-A-Budget Guide to London's Hidden Chic by Elle Ford

The Spell of the Horse: Stories of Healing & Personal Transformation with Nature's Finest Teachers by Pam Billinge

The #authorpower publishing company
Discovering outstanding authors
www.blackbird-books.com
2/25 Earls Terrace, London W8 6LP
@Blackbird_Bks

blackbird

226

CPSIA information can be obtained
at www.ICGtesting.com
Printed in the USA
BVHW030850301118
534434BV00001B/47/P

9 780995 473584